THE HOLOCAUST LIBRARY

The Final Solution

Lucent Books, P.O. Box 289011, San Diego, CA 92198-9011

Books in the Holocaust Library

The Death Camps
The Final Solution
The Nazis
Nazi War Criminals
The Resistance
The Righteous Gentiles
The Survivors

THE HOLOCAUST LIBRARY

The Final Solution

by

EARLE RICE JR.

Library of Congress Cataloging-in-Publication Data

Rice, Earle.
  The final solution / by Earle Rice Jr.
    p. cm. — (The Holocaust library)
  Includes bibliographical references and index.
  Summary: Discusses the origins, development, and implementation of the Final Solution, in which six million Jews were systematically exterminated by the Nazis during World War II.
  ISBN 1-56006-095-6 (alk. paper)
  1. Holocaust, Jewish (1939–1945)—Juvenile literature.
  [1. Holocaust, Jewish (1939–1945)] I. Title. II. Series:
Holocaust library (San Diego, Calif.)
D804.34.R53 1998
940.53'18—dc21   97-10847
                                                                 CIP
                                                                  AC

Copyright 1998 by Lucent Books, Inc., P.O. Box 289011,
San Diego, CA 92198-9011

Table of Contents

Foreword

More than eleven million innocent people, mostly Jews but also millions of others deemed "subhuman" by Adolf Hitler such as Gypsies, Russians, and Poles, were murdered by the Germans during World War II. The magnitude and unique horror of the Holocaust continues to make it a focal point in history—not only the history of modern times, but also the entire record of humankind. While the war itself temporarily changed the political landscape, the Holocaust forever changed the way we look at ourselves.

Starting with the European Renaissance in the 1400s, continuing through the Enlightenment of the 1700s, and extending to the Liberalism of the 1800s, philosophers and others developed the idea that people's intellect and reason allowed them to rise above their animal natures and conquer poverty, brutality, warfare, and all manner of evils. Given the will to do so, there was no height to which humanity might not rise. Was not mankind, these people argued, the noblest creation of God—in the words of the Bible, "a little lower than the angels"?

Western Europeans believed so heartily in these concepts that when rumors of mass murders by the Nazis began to emerge, people refused to accept—despite mounting evidence—that such things could take place. Even the Jews who were being deported to the death camps had a hard time believing that they were headed toward extermination. Rational beings, they argued, could not commit such actions. When the veil of secrecy was finally ripped from the death camps, however, the world recoiled in shock and horror. If humanity was capable of such depravity, what was its true nature? Were humans lower even than animals instead of just beneath the angels?

The perpetration of the Holocaust, so far outside the bounds of society's experience, cried out for explanations. For more than a half century, people have sought them. Thousands of books, diaries, sermons, poems, plays, films, and lectures have been devoted to almost every imaginable aspect of the Holocaust, yet it remains one of the most difficult episodes in history to understand.

Some scholars have explained the Holocaust as a uniquely German event, pointing to the racial supremacy theories of German philosophers, the rigidity of German society, and the tradition of obedience to authority. Others have seen it as a uniquely Jewish phenomenon, the culmination of centuries of anti-Semitism in Christian Europe. Still others have said that the Holocaust was a unique combination of these two factors—a set of circumstances unlikely ever to recur.

Such explanations are comfortable and simple—too simple. The Holocaust was neither a German event nor a Jewish event. It was a human event. The same forces—racism, prejudice, fanaticism—that sent millions to the gas chambers have not disappeared. If anything, they have become more evident. One cannot say, "It can't happen again." On a different scale, it has happened again. More than a million Cambodians were killed between 1974 and 1979 by a Communist government. In 1994 thousands of innocent civilians were murdered in tribal warfare between the Hutu and Tutsi tribes in the African nations of Burundi and Rwanda. Christian Serbs in Bosnia embarked on a program of "ethnic cleansing" in the mid-1990s, seeking to rid the country of Muslims.

The complete answer to the Holocaust has proved elusive. Indeed, it may never be found. The search, however, must continue. As author Elie Wiesel, a survivor of the death camps, wrote, "No one has the right to speak for the dead. . . . Still, the story had to be told. In spite of all risks, all possible misunderstandings. It needed to be told for the sake of our children."

Each book in Lucent Books' seven volume Holocaust Library covers a different topic that reveals the full gamut of human response to the Holocaust. *The Nazis, The Final Solution, The Death Camps*, and *Nazi War Criminals* focus on the perpetrators of the Holocaust and their plan to eliminate the Jewish people. Volumes on *The Righteous Gentiles, The Resistance*, and *The Survivors* reveal that humans are capable of being "the noblest creation of God," able to commit acts of bravery and altruism even in the most terrible circumstances.

History offers a way to interpret and reinterpret the past and an opportunity to alter the future. Lucent Books' topic-centered approach is an ideal introduction for students to study such phenomena as the Holocaust. After all, only by becoming knowledgeable about such atrocities can humanity hope to prevent future crimes from occurring. Although such historical lessons seem clear and unavoidable, as historian Yehuda Bauer wrote, "People seldom learn from history. Can we be an exception?"

Chronology of Events

1933

January The *Machtergreifung*, or seizure of power; German president Paul von Hindenburg appoints Adolf Hitler chancellor of the German Reich; the exclusion of Jews begins.

March 9 Hitler appoints Heinrich Himmler police president of Munich; Himmler subsequently establishes the first concentration camp at Dachau.

March 24 The Nazi-controlled Reichstag enacts the Enabling Law.

March 31 Hitler initiates the *Gleichschaltung*, or coordination, process, which forms a vital part of his consolidation of power.

April 1 Nazis boycott Jewish shops, offices, and businesses.

April 7 Enactment of anti-Jewish legislation commences.

April 26 Hermann Göring forms the Gestapo.

October 14 Hitler announces Germany's withdrawal from the League of Nations.

1934

June 29–30 The Night of the Long Knives; Himmler's SS purges the rival SA in a bloodbath ordered by Hitler.

1935

September 15 Hitler decrees the anti-Semitic Nuremberg Laws at the annual Nuremberg rally; the persecution of Jews begins.

1936

June 17 Hitler names Himmler chief of all German police.

September 9 Hitler introduces the Four-Year Plan at Nuremberg.

1937

November 5 The Hossbach Conference; Hitler reveals plans for aggressively expanding Germany's lebensraum (living space).

1938

March 12–13 Germany annexes Austria.

October 28 Germany deports between 17,000 and 18,000 Polish Jews.

November 7 Herschel Grynszpan, a young Polish Jew, mortally wounds Ernst vom Rath, a third secretary in the German embassy in Paris. Rath dies two days later.

November 9–10 *Kristallnacht*, or Night of the Broken Glass; Nazis rampage against Jews and Jewish establishments throughout Germany in retaliation for Rath's assassination.

1939

January 30 On the sixth anniversary of his accession to power, Hitler warns of the destruction of the Jewish race in Europe.

March 15 Germany annexes Czechoslovakia.

Summer Hitler authorizes the organization of a euthanasia program—code-named *Aktion T4*—for the methodical killing of mentally and physically handicapped children and adults.

September 1   German troops invade Poland; World War II and the expulsion of Jews begin.

September 21   RSHA chief Reinhard Heydrich issues orders to establish ghettos in Nazi-occupied Poland.

October   First ghetto established in Piotrków Trybunalski.

October 12   Hitler appoints Hans Frank to govern occupied Poland.

November 23   Jews ordered to wear identifying armbands.

November 28   Frank orders formation of Jewish councils (*Judenräte*).

1940

February   Ghetto established in Lodz.

June   Reserve Police Battalion 101 sent to Lodz to cleanse the area of Jews.

October 12   Ghetto established in Warsaw.

1941

March   Hitler issues the Commissar Decree authorizing the killing of Soviet commissars and others.

March 13   Field Marshal Keitel issues top-secret directive specifying "orders for special areas"; *Einsatzgruppen* (task forces) formed.

June 22   German troops invade Russia; the annihilation of Jews begins.

July 31   Göring directive orders Heydrich to proceed with plans for "the intended Final Solution of the Jewish question."

Summer   Hitler terminates euthanasia program.

Fall   Heydrich appoints Adolf Eichmann to head Jewish resettlement office.

September 29–30   Men of *Einsatzgruppe C* murder 33,771 people, mostly Jews, at Babi Yar.

December   The first death camp established at Chelmno.

December 8   Germans begin killing Jews and Gypsies from the Lodz ghetto.

1942

January 20   Heydrich convenes Wannsee Conference to work out details for implementing the Final Solution.

March   Death camp opens at Belzec; Auschwitz begins operations as a death camp.

May   Death camp opens at Sobibor.

June 4   Heydrich dies of wounds received in assassination attempt staged by Free Czech agents eight days earlier.

July   Death camp opens at Treblinka.

August   Majdanek begins operations as a death camp.

1943

November 3   Germans exterminate forty thousand Jews, most of them at Majdanek, during *Erntefest* (Harvest Festival).

1944

June 6   Allied forces invade Europe at Normandy.

November   Himmler orders crematoria at Auschwitz destroyed; camp evacuations and death marches commence.

1945

January 27   Red Army troops enter Auschwitz; the liberation of concentration camps begins and continues until the end of the war.

May 8   World War II in Europe and the Holocaust end.

November 20   War crimes trials begin at Nuremberg; trials continue elsewhere to this day.

Explaining the Holocaust

During World War II the Germans slaughtered millions of innocent Europeans—Jews, Gypsies, Slavs, and others, as well as untold thousands of mentally and physically challenged individuals. The Germans' crime of mass extermination was so great and ghastly as to require the invention of a new word to define it: *genocide*.

Coined in 1944 by Professor Raphael Lemkin of Duke University, the term derived from the Greek *genos*, race, and the Latin *coedere*, to kill. It is defined as the deliberate and systematic destruction of a racial, political, or cultural group. The word was first applied solely to the attempted extermination of six million Jews in Germany's Third Reich. Its implementation formed the defining part of German chancellor Adolf Hitler's "final solution to the Jewish question,"[1] a policy dedicated to maintaining the purity of "Aryan-Nordic-Germanic blood" through a program of "blood, selection, and austerity."[2] Over time the use of the term *genocide* became more generalized and was expanded to include the additional millions of Europeans victimized by the German scourge.

Today the physical destruction of some six million Jews during the Second World War is better known as the Holocaust (from the Greek words *holos*, whole, and *kaustos*, burnt). Although the Final Solution (*Die Endlösung*), a German euphemism, is often used interchangeably with the Holocaust, the gentler phrasing does nothing to alter the consummate evil inherent in the act it names.

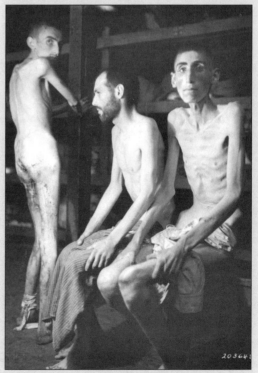

Men in the final stages of starvation stare in mute testament to the horrors of the Final Solution.

Anti-Semitism

Anti-Semitism, that is, hostility toward or discrimination against Jews as a religious or racial group, did not, of course, originate with Hitler and his disciples in Germany's Third Reich. The roots of anti-Semitism extend back for centuries in Europe. Louis L. Snyder, one of the eminent historians of German World War II history and lore, writes that anti-Semitism is the

> name first applied to a movement of opposition to Jews in the second half of the nineteenth century. Anti-Semitism had been prevalent, however, throughout Europe in the Middle Ages and varied in intensity in different countries. The modern movement originated in Russia and Central Europe, which had large Jewish minorities. Antipathy toward Jews in its recent form was not due completely to their religion but was based on economic factors of wealth and power. Toward the latter part of the nineteenth century, anti-Semitism assumed a virulent form in imperial Russia and Hungary, where there were riots and murders. The publication of the *Protocols of the Elders of Zion* [a forged polemic based on an earlier diatribe against Napoleon and used by Hitler in his campaign against the Jews] in the early twentieth century stimulated pogroms (attacks on Jews). Anti-Semitic political parties rose in Austria and Germany, and efforts were made to restrict the political rights of Jews.

> A revival of anti-Semitism swept through Germany as soon as Hitler assumed political power. Jews, no matter what their class or reputation, were reviled and deprived of their livelihood. Germans of part-Jewish origin were included in the persecutions. Nazi anti-Semitism took the form of a political movement after Hitler promoted it as a basic part of his personal philosophy. . . . Hitler made anti-Semitism an official movement in the Third Reich. Nazi anti-Semitism led to the slaughter of 6 million Jews in the concentration camps and the extermination camps.[3]

Perhaps no single event has been so thoroughly studied, dissected, analyzed, diagnosed, put back together, and written about in the past half-century as the Holocaust. Yet today, some fifty-plus years after the tragedy ended, scholars and laypeople alike continue to debate its whys, hows, and wherefores.

The Revisionists

In more recent years, a small but insistent fringe element of so-called history revisionists extends the credibility envelope to the point of claiming that the Holocaust, in fact, never happened. But tens of thousands of survivors of Hitler's death camps, untold thousands of liberating Allied soldiers, and tons of documentary and photographic evidence attest to the reality of the Nazis' attempt to exterminate an entire race of people. Thus, the revisionists and their arguments warrant little additional comment other than to echo the words of Professor Klaus P. Fischer: "These [the revisionists] must be grouped with the sort of persons who insist that America never really went to the moon, that it was all a deception staged in some Hollywood studio."[4] In a word, "specious" best describes revisionist disclaimers. Much legitimate controversy continues to surround the Holocaust, however, regarding its origins, development, and implementation.

Three Schools of Thought

In general, conventional Holocaust theorists are categorized as belonging to one of three schools of thought: (1) the "intentionalists," (2) the "functionalists" (also referred to as "structuralists"), and (3) the "eclectics."

The intentionalists view the Holocaust as a manifestation of Hitler's anti-Semitism. They maintain that the Germans' mass slaughter of the Jews evolved directly and predictably from Hitler's hateful anti-Semitic philosophy and from the totalitarian policies espoused by the Nazis since the inception of the Nazi Party in 1920. Thus, say the intentionalists, Hitler and the Nazis *intended* from the start to annihilate the Jews.

The functionalists, on the other hand, tend to minimize Hitler's role. They argue that the mass extermination program was more the product of a bureaucracy functioning out of control than of a long-held intent on the part of Hitler and the Nazis to reach a "final solution to the Jewish question." The functionalists, therefore, focus on the dynamic political and economic situation in Germany during the 1930s. And they perceive the Holocaust as the result of the Nazi regime's chaotic decision-making process, rather than as the culmination of Adolf Hitler's lifelong passion.

The eclectics embrace a third and more recent school of thought on the Nazis' murderous program. They accept the more positive elements of both preceding schools, while discarding the less defensible assertions of their predecessors. Accordingly, the eclectics support the functionalists' contention that at the start the Nazis held only a very general goal of ridding Germany of Jews, called *Entjudung* ("de-Judaization").

It is true that the concept of *Die Endlösung* (the Final Solution) surfaced only after other solutions were tried and fell short of

Genocide and Anti-Semitism

Historian of Jewish history Lucy S. Dawidowicz, in her classic work *The War Against the Jews, 1933–1945*, clearly believes that the roots of genocide grew out of the fertile soil of Adolf Hitler's anti-Semitism:

> The structuralist interpretation fails to convince because it takes no account of ideas and intentions, even such monstrous ones as Hitler's. For history begins in the minds of men and women, in the ideas they hold and in the decisions they make. "Every idea," Oliver Holmes wrote in a judicial opinion, "is an incitement." History renders an account not only of battles and wars, elections and revolutions, intrigues and alliances, but above all of the ideas, ambitions, and goals of the people who set these events in motion.
>
> The English historian and philosopher R. G. Collingwood made the distinction between the outside and the inside of an event. The outside of the event, he said, was its action; the inside was the thought of the agent of the action. To penetrate the inside of the event, the historian has to enter the minds of the men and women whose actions make history and in effect recreate their thoughts. The minds of these agents of history are, to the historian, as important as any battlefield or house of parliament. They are far and away the most strategic sites of history.

Although many Germans were anti-Semitic before Hitler came to power, anti-Semitism became an institution under his reign. Here, a page from a children's picture book compares the physical traits and attributes of Germans and Jews.

desired results. But it is also true that the goals of both *Entjudung* and the dehumanizing anti-Jew doctrines of *Die Endlösung* were unswervingly adhered to for the entire existence of the Nazi Party.

A Fourth Explanation

The latest—and certainly the most provocative—attempt to explain the genocidal phenomenon can be found in Daniel Jonah Goldhagen's provocative book *Hitler's Willing Executioners: Ordinary Germans and the Holocaust*. Goldhagen, an assistant professor of government and social studies at Harvard University, introduced a fourth school of thought on the much-studied cataclysm. "Explaining why the Holocaust occurred," he writes, "requires a radical revision of what has until now been written." Goldhagen argues:

Germans' antisemitic beliefs about Jews were the central causal agent of the Holocaust. They were the central causal agent not only of Hitler's decision to annihilate European Jewry (which is accepted by many) but also of the perpetrators' willingness to kill and brutalize Jews. . . .

For the extermination of the Jews to occur, four principal things were necessary:

1. The Nazis—that is, the leadership, specifically Hitler—had to decide to undertake the extermination.

2. They had to gain control over the Jews, namely over the territory in which they resided.

3. They had to organize the extermination and devote to it sufficient resources.

4. They had to induce a large number of people to carry out the killings.[5]

Much has been written about the first three elements, but little of the fourth, which, when written about at all, has been treated only "perfunctorily and mainly by assumption."[6] Goldhagen, then, for the first time, dared to lay an ample share of the blame for the mass executions squarely on the shoulders of ordinary Germans. The debate continues.

Phases, Time Periods, and Human Elements

Irrespective of their differences, historians generally agree with L. S. Snyder that the Nazi anti-Semitic policy was carried out in four phases: (1) exclusion; (2) persecution; (3) expulsion; and (4) annihilation; and that it was spread across four time periods, as noted by Abraham J. and Hershel Edelheit:

"No Germans, No Holocaust"

In *Hitler's Willing Executioners*, one of the more recent books attempting to explain the Holocaust, Daniel Jonah Goldhagen, an assistant professor of government and social studies at Harvard University, became perhaps the first historian to place most of the blame for "the most shocking event of the century" on ordinary Germans. Goldhagen forcibly asserts that it is necessary to focus on the people who gave life to the "inert institutional forms," and who "peopled the institutions of genocidal killing," to understand the Holocaust. He states:

These people were overwhelmingly and most importantly Germans. While members of other national groups aided the Germans in their slaughter of Jews, the commission of the Holocaust was primarily a German undertaking. Non-Germans were not essential to the perpetration of the genocide, and they did not supply the drive and initiative that pushed it forward. To be sure, had the Germans not found European (especially, Eastern European) helpers, then the Holocaust would have unfolded somewhat differently, and the Germans would likely not have succeeded in killing as many Jews. Still, this was above all a German enterprise; the decisions, plans, organizational resources, and the majority of its executors were Germans. Comprehension and explanation of the perpetration of the Holocaust therefore requires an explanation of the *Germans'* drive to kill Jews. Because what can be said about the Germans cannot be said about any other nationality or about all of the other nationalities combined—namely no Germans, no Holocaust—the focus [in Goldhagen's book] is appropriately on the German perpetrators.

Hitler is surrounded by fervent admirers proffering the "Heil, Hitler" salute. Some scholars say that Hitler merely capitalized on the already virulent anti-Semitism of the average German.

1. From the *Machtergreifung* (Seizure of Power) on January 30, 1933, to the Nuremberg rallies of September 15, 1935;

2. From the Nuremberg rallies to the outbreak of World War II on September 1, 1939;

3. From the outbreak of war to the invasion of the Soviet Union on June 22, 1941; and

4. From the invasion of the Soviet Union to the end of World War II in Europe on May 8, 1945.[7]

The growth of the Holocaust field of studies has also encouraged the development of "three basic subdivisions or areas of specialization that focus respectively on the perpetrators, the victims, and the bystanders."[8]

Unparalleled Evil

What follows is the story of the Final Solution, as conceived and orchestrated by Adolf Hitler and as faithfully implemented by his followers. Their evil deeds remain unparalleled in world history and perhaps beyond the ability of mere mortals to ever fully comprehend. This tale of supreme wickedness begins in the village of Braunau, on the Inn River between Austria and Germany.

CHAPTER 1

The Roots of Genocide

Adolf Hitler—*the single individual most responsible for the destruction of Europe's Jews*—was born of German descent in Braunau on April 20, 1889. He grew up in Leonding on the Danube, near Linz, Austria. After an unexceptional childhood, he left home at the age of eighteen and moved to Vienna, where he hoped to make his mark in the world as an artist.

He applied for entrance to the Academy of Fine Arts in the summer of 1907, but his dream of becoming an artist began to fade when he failed the entrance examination. Refusing to give up on his dream, he sat again for the examination in the autumn of 1908 and failed again. The rector of the academy reportedly told him that his real talent lay in architecture. Hitler's second failure shook him to the core of his being.

Hitler spent the next five years living off sparse earnings and charity, drifting aimlessly among the city's homeless and destitute. "Five years in which I was forced to earn a living, first as a day laborer, then as a painter," he wrote later in his rambling, semiliterate autobiography *Mein Kampf (My Struggle)*, "a truly meager living which never sufficed to appease even my daily hunger. Hunger was then my faithful bodyguard."[9]

And it was in Vienna, while coming of age amid hardships and squalor, that Adolf Hitler nurtured the doctrines of race and class hatred that would shape his destiny and ultimately result in the deaths of millions.

The Jewish Question

Vienna, capital of the Austro-Hungarian empire and hub of banking, finance, fashion, and culture under the Hapsburg dynasty, counted nearly two hundred thousand Jews among its two million inhabitants. Hitler professed to having harbored no ill feelings toward Jews prior to his arrival there. Although he may have experienced a hint of anti-Semitism while growing up in Leonding or in nearby Linz, it is doubtful that he encountered there more than a few Jews to fit the image of his later fanaticism. But August Kubizek, a boyhood companion, recalled that in Linz "his anti-Semitism was already pronounced. . . . Hitler was already a confirmed anti-Semite when he went to Vienna. And although his experiences in Vienna might have deepened this feeling, they certainly did not give birth to it."[10] Without regard to the inceptive moment of his anti-Semitism, it can be said with certainty that in Vienna Hitler came in close contact with more Jews and Communists than he ever had previously.

As to what motivated Hitler's impassioned hatred for Jews, historians can only

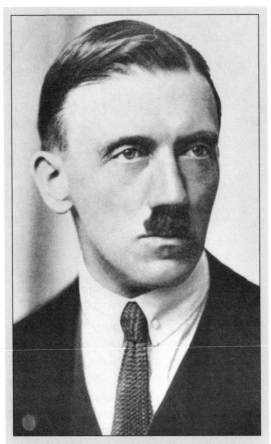

Hitler began formulating his especially violent form of anti-Semitism as a young man.

Hitler substantially educated himself in what was to become his lifelong anti-Semitic philosophy. "Anti-Semitism, in fact, was the oxygen of Hitler's political life," writes Klaus P. Fischer. "Once it had crystallized, it remained a permanent feature of his character, increasing steadily in virulence up to his final moments in his underground tomb beneath the Reich chancellery."[12]

One of Hitler's first meetings with a Jew in Vienna's Inner City left such a lasting impression on the future dictator that he later wrote about it in *Mein Kampf:*

> I suddenly encountered an apparition in a black caftan and black sidelocks. Is this a Jew? was my first thought.
>
> For, to be sure, they had not looked like that in Linz. I observed the man furtively and cautiously, but the longer I stared at this foreign face, scrutinizing feature for feature, the more my first question assumed a new form:
>
> Is this a German?[13]

Following this experience, Hitler purchased several anti-Semitic pamphlets in an effort to learn more about Jews, supposedly hoping to dispel his doubts as to whether they were really German.

"Unfortunately, they all proceeded from the supposition that in principle the reader knew or even understood the Jewish question to a certain degree,"[14] he wrote. (It is interesting to note that he was already using the phrase "the Jewish question.")

"Like a Maggot in a Rotten Body"

At first Hitler averred he found the anti-Semitic rhetoric ill-founded and chose not to believe it. But as his research into Jews as Germans deepened, and his contact with

speculate. "Despite the wealth of information gained from an analysis of all of the available data on Hitler's medical, intellectual and social backgrounds," according to Werner Maser, one of Hitler's many biographers, "there is still no satisfactory explanation of his anti-Semitism."[11]

While in Vienna, Hitler studied the political techniques of Karl Lueger, Vienna's popular mayor. And he absorbed the crackpot racial ideas of two demagogic anti-Semites—Lanz von Liebenfels, a defrocked monk, and Georg von Schoerner, the Austrian Pan-German leader. But it appears that them increased, he began to think of them not as Germans but as a separate people:

> Wherever I went, I began to see Jews, and the more I saw, the more sharply they became distinguished in my eyes from the rest of humanity. Particularly, the Inner City and the districts north of the Danube Canal swarmed with a people which even outwardly had lost all resemblance to Germans.[15]

Hitler went on to criticize the attitude of the Jews themselves. A small faction of Jews advocated Zionism—an international movement to establish a Jewish state in Palestine (now Israel). But the liberal majority of Jews, though opposed to Zionism as a dangerous way of expressing their Jewishness, did not openly reject their Zionist brethren as Hitler thought they should:

> In a short time this apparent struggle between Zionistic and liberal Jews disgusted me; for it was false through and through, founded on lies and scarcely in keeping with the moral elevation and purity always claimed by these people.[16]

Hitler had barely begun to denigrate the Jews. His criticisms grew baser with each paragraph:

> The cleanliness of this people, moral and otherwise, I must say, is a point itself. By their very exterior you could tell that these were no lovers of water, and, to your distress, you often knew it with your eyes closed. Later I often grew sick to my stomach from the smell of these caftan-wearers. Added to this, there was their unclean dress and their generally unheroic appearance.

All this could scarcely be called very attractive; but it became positively repulsive when, in addition to their physical uncleanliness, you discovered the moral stains on this "chosen people."[17]

With the rambling redundancy characteristic of *Mein Kampf*, Hitler continued for page after page to condemn every conceivable aspect of Jewishness. He tried to suggest to the reader that he had observed the Jews with an open mind. He implied that his criticisms (and ultimately his hatred) for Jews had formed as his knowledge of them increased. The Jews, the reader might readily infer, had *earned* his revulsion:

> In a short time I was made more thoughtful than ever by my slowly rising insight into the type of activity carried on by the Jews in certain fields.

> Was there any form of filth or profligacy [depravity], particularly in cultural life, without at least one Jew involved in it?

> If you cut even cautiously into such an abscess, you found, like a maggot in a rotten body, often dazzled by the sudden light—a kike![18]

Hitler's hateful anti-Jew polemic, written several years after his Vienna period, meandered on to elaborate on the evils of the Jew-dominated press and Jews engaged in public artistic life.

On Parting a Jew from His Opinion

Hitler's self-declared initial tolerance for Jews and their ways soon dissolved in a wash of self-induced distortions attributing all of Germany's ills to a malignant Jewish-Marxist conspiracy:

The fact that nine tenths of all literary filth, artistic trash, and theatrical idiocy can be set to the account of a people [the Jews], constituting hardly one hundredth of all the country's inhabitants, could not be talked away; it was the plain truth.[19]

As for the press and other publications, he wrote:

The objectivity of exposition now seemed to me more akin to lies than honest truth; and the writers were—Jews. . . .

The transfigured raptures of their theatrical critics were always directed at Jewish writers, and their disapproval never struck anyone but Germans. . . . The

trashy content of the short story now appeared to me as outright indecency, and in the language I detected the accents of a foreign people; the sense of the whole thing was so obviously hostile to Germanism, that this could only have been intentional.[20]

Hitler's probings led him to perceive the Jew as begetter of all things that afflicted or threatened Germans and Germany. He saw Jews as purveyors of prostitution, directors of Social Democracy (deemed Marxists by Hitler), publishers of Marxist propaganda, representatives of government and labor unions, and even as street agitators. And his inquiries into Jews and their activities led him inevitably to a passionate interest in politics.

In the following passage, Hitler revealed telling aspects not only of his anti-Semitism but of the political acumen that he would so successfully employ later:

I took all the Social Democratic pamphlets I could lay hands on and sought the names of their authors: Jews. . . . One thing had grown clear to me: the party with whose petty representatives I had been carrying on the most violent struggle for months was, as to leadership, almost exclusively in the hands of a foreign people; for, to my deep and joyful satisfaction, I had at last come to the conclusion that the Jew was no German.

Only now did I become thoroughly acquainted with the seducer of our people.

A single year of my sojourn in Vienna had sufficed to imbue me with the conviction that no worker could be so stubborn that he would not in the end succumb to better knowledge and better explanations. Slowly I had become an

The front page from a 1934 edition of the anti-Semitic newspaper Der Stürmer. *Featured is an article that accuses Jews of causing a number of German ills.*

In Dubious Battle

As a young man in Vienna, Adolf Hitler developed an all-consuming hatred for Jews and subsequently an equally compelling aversion to Marxists (Communists). He later recounted his awakening to his perceived threat of Social Democracy (Marxism) in *Mein Kampf*, an autobiographical discourse on his formative years and emerging anti-Semitic and political tenets:

> I began to make myself familiar with the founders of this [Social Democratic] doctrine, in order to study the foundations of the movement. If I reached my goal more quickly than at first I had ventured to believe, it was thanks to my newly acquired, though at the time not very profound, knowledge of the Jewish question. . . .

> For me this was the time for the greatest spiritual upheaval I have ever had to go through.

> I had ceased to be a weak-kneed cosmopolitan and become an anti-Semite. . . .

As I delved more deeply into the teachings of Marxism and thus in tranquil clarity submitted the deeds of the Jewish people to contemplation, Fate itself gave me its answer. . . .

If, with the help of his Marxist creed, the Jew is victorious over the other peoples of the world, his crown will be the funeral wreath of humanity and this planet will, as it did thousands [changed to "millions" in the second edition] of years ago, move through the ether devoid of men.

Eternal Nature inexorably avenges the infringement of her commands.

Hence today I believe that I am acting in accordance with the will of the Almighty Creator: *by defending myself against the Jew, I am fighting for the work of the Lord.*

The last emphasis is Hitler's and warrants no additional comment.

---

expert in their own [Marxist] doctrine and used it as a weapon in the struggle for my own profound conviction [which culminated in National Socialism, that is to say, Nazism]. . . . The great masses could be saved, if only with the gravest sacrifice in time and patience.

But a Jew could never be parted from his opinions.[21]

Intentionalists might conclude from this that Hitler was even then convinced that death was the only sure solution for parting a Jew from his opinion.

"The Anti-Semitism of Reason"

Hitler left Vienna for Munich in May 1913. When World War I broke out in August 1914, he enlisted in the Sixteenth Bavarian Infantry Regiment, rather than joining the Austrian army and risk having to serve with the likes of Vienna's Jews. He distinguished himself at the front as a dispatch runner, earning the Iron Cross, First and Second Class, while suffering two wounds and a severe gassing near the end of the war.

After five years of failure and disappointment in Vienna, Hitler's war service instilled in him a sense of a new beginning, a new purpose

Hitler (front row, far left) poses with other members of his unit during World War I. While serving in the Sixteenth Bavarian Infantry Regiment, Hitler distinguished himself as a soldier and earned the coveted Iron Cross.

in life. He survived the war and came out of it believing that destiny had spared him to rescue a humbled Germany from the fetters of the Versailles treaty and the corrupt influence of Jews and Marxists. And he recognized that Germany's salvation and redemption—not to mention his own ascendance to power—could only be achieved through politics.

On September 16, 1919, Hitler, while still a corporal in the postwar German army, joined the German Workers' Party (*Deutsche Arbeiterpartei*, or DAP) as member Number 55. A short time later he was named Number 7 of its Executive Committee. He "soon changed its name to the National Socialist German Workers' Party [*Nationalsozialistische Deutsche Arbeiterpartei*, NSDAP—or later "Nazi"—for short] and had imposed himself as its Chairman by July 1921," writes Robert S. Wistrich, the *Jewish Chronicle* Professor of Jewish History at University College, London. Hitler left the army to pursue a career in politics. It was then, Wistrich notes, that

Hitler discovered a powerful talent for oratory as well as giving the new party its symbol—the swastika—and its greeting "Heil!" His hoarse, grating voice, for all the bombastic, humorless, histrionic content of his speeches, dominated audiences by dint of his tone of impassioned conviction and gift for self-dramatization.[22]

Hitler became führer of the then 3,000-member party in November 1921 and, writes Wistrich, "focused his propaganda against the Versailles Treaty, the 'November criminals' [German leaders responsible for concluding the armistice on November 11, 1918], and the visible, internal enemy No. 1, the 'Jew', who was responsible for all Germany's domestic problems."[23]

Wistrich recalls Hitler's Twenty-Five Point program for the newly formed Nazi Party, announced on February 24, 1920, in which

the exclusion of Jews from the *Volk* community [*Volk* is German for "people"; the Nazis used the term to connote a community of pure blood], the myth of Aryan race supremacy, and extreme nationalism were combined with "socialistic" ideas of profit-sharing and nationalization inspired

Hitler mesmerizes a small audience in the 1920s. A powerful speaker, Hitler was able to motivate others to action.

The Road to Auschwitz

"Hitler's campaign to annihilate the Jews was not a sudden whim," writes Leni Yahil in *The Holocaust: The Fate of European Jewry*. "From the inception of his political career, the struggle against the Jews had been a prominent component of his Weltanschauung [worldview] and political method."

More recently, plainspoken Harvard historian Daniel Jonah Goldhagen bore out Yahil's observations. In *Hitler's Willing Executioners: Ordinary Germans and the Holocaust*, the young and controversial professor of government and social studies writes:

The idea that death and death alone is the only fitting punishment for Jews was publicly articulated by Hitler at the beginning of his political career on August 13, 1920, in a speech entirely devoted to anti-Semitism, "Why Are We Antisemites?" In the middle of that speech, the still politically obscure Hitler suddenly digressed to the subject of the death sentence and why it ought to be applied to Jews. Healthy elements of a nation, he declared, know that "criminals guilty of crimes against the nation, i.e., parasites on the national community," cannot be tolerated, that under certain circumstances they must be punished only with death, since imprisonment lacks the quality of irrevocableness. "The heaviest bolt is not heavy enough and the securest prison is not secure enough that *a few million* could not in the end open it. Only one bolt cannot be opened—*and that is death*" [Goldhagen's emphasis]. This was not a casual utterance, but reflected an idea and resolve that had already ripened and taken root in Hitler's mind.

In the discussion that ensued with members of the audience about the above-mentioned speech, Hitler revealed that he had contemplated the question of how the "Jewish problem" is to be solved. He resolved to be thoroughgoing. "We have, however, decided that we shall not come with ifs, ands, and buts, but when the matter comes to a solution, it will be done thoroughly." In the speech proper, Hitler spelled out, with a candid explicitness that he prudently would not repeat in public after he achieved national prominence, what he meant by the phrase "it will be done thoroughly." It meant that putting the entire Jewish nation to death—or, as Hitler himself had stated publicly a few months earlier in another speech, "to seize the Evil [the Jews] by the roots and exterminate it root and branch"—would be the most just and effective punishment, the only enduring "solution." Mere imprisonment would be too clement a penalty for such world-historical criminals and one, moreover, fraught with danger, since the Jews could one day emerge from their prisons and resume their evil ways. Hitler's maniacal conception of the Jews, his consuming hatred of them, and his natural murderous propensity rendered him incapable of becoming reconciled permanently to any "solution of the Jewish Problem" save that of extinction.

The road to Auschwitz [the largest Nazi death camp] was not twisted. Conceived by Hitler's apocalyptically bent mind as an urgent, though future, project, its completion had to wait until conditions were right.

24   **The Final Solution**

by ideologues like Gottfried Feder [an early economics adviser to Hitler]. Hitler's first written utterance on political questions dating from this period emphasized that what he called "the anti-semitism of reason" must lead "to the systematic combating and elimination of Jewish privileges. Its ultimate goal must implacably be the total removal of the Jews."[24]

Such recommendations, coming so early in Hitler's political life, cannot but help to lend credence to the intentionalists' position that Hitler intended from the start to eliminate the Jews.

A Handbook for Revolution

The Nazi Party grew rapidly. Heady with his newfound authority, Hitler then attempted to move too fast up the ladder of political prominence. On the night of November 8, 1923, during a speech by Bavarian state commissioner Gustav Ritter von Kahr at Munich's *Bürgerbräukeller* (an expansive beer hall), Hitler led six hundred Nazis and right-wing followers into a gathering of about three thousand Germans.

Leaping onto a table and waving a pistol wildly, he fired a shot into the ceiling and shouted, "The National Revolution has begun!" He then herded Kahr and two other Bavarian officials into an adjoining room at pistol point. Leaving them in the custody of cohorts, Hitler returned to the main hall and boomed to the crowd: "The Bavarian Ministry is removed!" He told them that the first task of his new government would be "to organize the march on that sinful Babel, Berlin, and save the German people. Tomorrow will find either a national government in Germany or us dead."[25]

Hitler was right only to a point. His attempted coup was quickly put down by local police. In the aftermath of the Beer Hall Putsch, as his failed coup became known, sixteen Nazis and three policemen lay dead in the streets of Munich. A number of others were wounded, including Hermann Göring, the future number-two Nazi under Hitler. For Hitler's role in the fracas, a court sentenced him to five years' imprisonment for high treason, of which he served only nine months at Landsberg am Lech.

"On the surface the Beer-Hall *Putsch* seemed to be a failure," observes Louis L. Snyder, "but actually it was a brilliant achievement for a political nobody." Snyder writes:

Hitler strikes a dramatic pose as he looks out from his cell at Landsberg prison.

In a few hours Hitler catapulted his scarcely known, unimportant movement into headlines throughout Germany and the world. Moreover, he learned an important lesson: direct action was not the way to political power. It was necessary that he seek political victory by winning the masses to his side and also by attracting the support of wealthy industrialists. Then he could ease his way to political supremacy by legal means. [26]

While serving his abbreviated sentence at Landsberg, Hitler used the time to good advantage. He dictated the first version of *Mein Kampf* to Emil Maurice, an early crony, and Rudolf Hess, another Putsch participant and fellow prisoner who, like Göring, would climb to the top of the Nazi hierarchy. Featuring a predominant theme of racial purity and Aryan supremacy, *Mein Kampf* represented a virtual handbook for revolution. It soon grew to be regarded as the bible of National Socialism.

In his crudely written autobiography, Hitler played on all the dissatisfactions of a defeated people, forewarning Germany and the world of his intentions. Few readers of

Posters advertise Mein Kampf, *the autobiography Hitler wrote while serving his sentence at Landsberg prison. Crudely written, the book focused on Hitler's revolutionary ideas.*

that time believed Hitler intended to carry out all the details of his boldly stated program for restoring German pride and Germany's prominence as a nation. They were wrong.

Deadly Fruit

In the 1928 elections, the Nazi Party won only twelve seats in the Reichstag (German parliament). But hard times came to the aid of Hitler and the National Socialists with the onset of the Great Depression. A newly resurgent German economy faltered when loan sources dried up. Exports declined sharply. Banks and factories closed. Unemployment soared. Bread lines formed. And Adolf Hitler happily welcomed the deprivations. "Never in my life," he wrote, "have I been so well disposed and inwardly contented as in these days. For hard reality has opened the eyes of millions of Germans."[27]

In the throes of Germany's despair, Hitler saw opportunity. "To a desperate Germany," writes Robert Edwin Herzstein, "Hitler offered crude solutions." Herzstein briefly recounts several:

> He would unilaterally end reparations and refuse to pay the debts incurred by Schacht [president of the Reichsbank, the national bank of Germany]; he would crush the Jew, whose greed was the cause of all economic evil; he would provide every German with food and a job. He promised nonpartisan politics, a Germany where people worked together, a Germany to be proud of.[28]

In 1930 the Nazis sent 107 deputies to the Reichstag. Two years later they won 230 seats. And as Germany entered the new year of 1933, the portal of power opened wide to Hitler and the Nazis.

Of those responsible for Hitler's and the Nazis' rapid rise to power, journalist William L. Shirer would later write:

> No class or group or party in Germany could escape its share of responsibility for the abandonment of the democratic [Weimar] Republic and the advent of Adolf Hitler. The cardinal error of the Germans who opposed Nazism was their failure to unite against it. . . . But the 63 per cent of the German people who expressed their opposition to Hitler were much too divided and shortsighted to combine against a common danger which they must have known would overwhelm them unless they united, however temporarily, to stamp it out.[29]

But the German majority demonstrated no such unity. The gnarled roots of genocide were by then deeply entrenched in the Nazi psyche and doctrine. And while a complacent nation looked on, the roots began to sprout their deadly fruit.

2

The *Machtergreifung:* The Seizure of Power

Germany entered the new and fateful year of 1933 beset by a deteriorating political situation. Three factions were vying for control of the economically depressed nation—the Prussian landed aristocracy in the east, the wealthy industrialists in the west, and the Reichswehr (the standing army at that time). In a move toward political compromise, Field Marshal Paul von Hindenburg, the eighty-six-year-old president of the Weimar Republic, reluctantly appointed Adolf Hitler as Germany's new chancellor.

"The German Revolution Has Begun!"

Shortly before noon on January 20, 1933, Hitler emerged from the German chancellery in Berlin and a roar went up from the crowd lining the snowy street outside. Foreign correspondent William L. Shirer writes:

> The man with the Charlie Chaplin mustache, who had been a down-and-out tramp in Vienna in his youth, an unknown soldier of World War I, a derelict in Munich in the first grim post-war days, the somewhat comical leader of the Beer Hall Putsch, this spellbinder who was not even German but Austrian, and who was only forty-three years old, had just been administered the oath as

Chancellor of the German Reich.[30]

Only moments earlier Hitler had sworn:

> I will employ my strength for the welfare of the German people, protect the constitution and laws of the German people, conscientiously discharge the duties imposed on me and conduct my affairs of office impartially and with justice for everyone.[31]

Historian Lucy S. Dawidowicz sharply and summarily rejects Hitler's sincerity:

> When Hitler uttered those words, he had already laid plans to destroy the constitution and the laws he was swearing to protect. Exercising neither impartiality nor justice, he was about to conduct relentless war on his enemies—democracy, freedom, parliamentarianism [rule by a cabinet form of government], political pluralism [independent participation in politics by diverse groups within common limits], and, above all, the Jews, the embodiment of everything he hated.[32]

But on that pivotal day in history, few could foresee what lay ahead for Germany and the Jews.

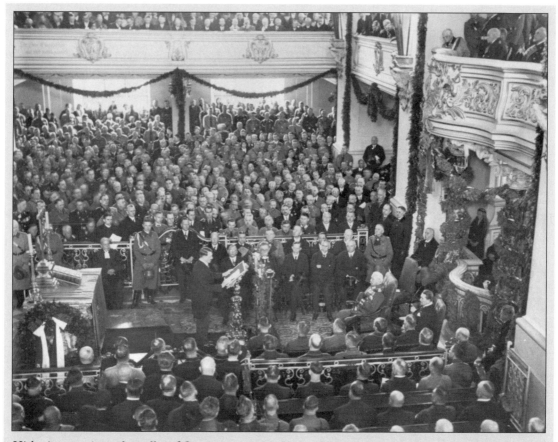

Hitler is sworn in as chancellor of Germany in 1933. He would use the position to propel himself into one of even more power.

That evening, from an upstairs window of the chancellery, Hans Frank, a lawyer and loyal Nazi who would later serve as governor-general of occupied Poland, stood behind Hitler and watched a spectacular procession of storm troopers tramping past in the street below. Long afterward, shortly before he was hanged at Nuremberg as a war criminal, Frank recalled, "God knows our hearts were pure that day, and if anyone had told us of the events to come, no one would have believed it, least of all I. It was a day of glory and happiness."[33]

William L. Shirer describes the spectacle like this:

From dusk until far past midnight the delirious Nazi storm troopers marched in a massive torchlight parade to celebrate the victory. By the tens of thousands, they emerged in disciplined columns from the depths of the Tiergarten [zoo], passed under the triumphal arch of the Brandenburg Gate and down the Wilhelmstrasse, their bands blaring the old martial airs to the thunderous beating of the drums, their voices bawling the new Horst Wessel song [the official marching song of the Nazi Party] and other tunes that were as old as Germany, their jack boots beating a mighty rhythm on the pavement, their torches held high and forming a ribbon of flame that illuminated the night and kindled the hurrahs of the onlookers massed on the sidewalks.[34]

Not everyone viewed the spectacle with happy feelings. France's ambassador, André François-Poncet, wrote, "The river of fire flowed past the French Embassy, whence, with heavy heart and filled with foreboding, I watched its luminous wake."[35]

Before retiring after three the next morning, exhausted but exhilarated, Joseph Goebbels, Reich propaganda leader of the Nazi Party, wrote in his diary: "It is almost like a dream . . . a fairy tale. . . . The new Reich has been born. Fourteen years of work have been crowned with victory. The German revolution has begun!"[36] And with it, the exclusion of the Jews from German life during the first phase of the Germans' war against the Jews.

The Enabling Law

In the subsequent March 5 election, the Nazi Party at last gained a majority in the Reichstag. With a 52-seat assist from the Nationalists (right-wing conservatives), the Nazis took control of 340 seats—a bare 17-seat majority.

Almost a decade earlier, after his unsuccessful attempt to take over the government by force in a Munich beer hall, Hitler vowed to achieve his goal in the future in a constitutional way. With his appointment as chancellor and with a new Nazi majority in the Reichstag, he had kept his promise. But much work remained to be done before he would become the all-powerful, undisputed dictator of Germany. Accordingly, Hitler set out at once to consolidate his power. The first

Once Hitler succeeded in passing the Enabling Law—which gave him power to enact laws without the cooperation of the Reichstag—he was on his way to becoming Germany's dictator.

important milestone on his path to sovereign supremacy was set in place on March 24, 1933, with the enactment of the Enabling Law.

"Hitler's dictatorship rested on the constitutional foundation of a single law: the so-called Enabling Law, *Gesetz zur Behebung der Not von Völk und Reich* (Law for Removing the Distress of People and Reich)," writes Alan Bullock, one of the more highly regarded of Hitler's many biographers. Continuing, Bullock notes the far-reaching powers inherent in the law:

The Enabling Bill which was laid before the House on 23 March 1933 gave the Government the power for four years to enact laws without the cooperation of the Reichstag. It specifically stated that this power should include the right to deviate from the Constitution and to conclude treaties with foreign states. It also provided that laws to be enacted by the Government should be drafted by the Chancellor, and should come into effect on the day after publication.[37]

Legislators arriving at the Reichstag to vote on the bill that day had to pass through a solid ring of black-shirted SS men encircling the building's exterior. (The SS, or *Schutzstaffel*, literally "defense echelon," was an elite unit originally formed as Hitler's personal guard. It was later transformed by its leader, Heinrich Himmler, into a massive force with which resided the ultimate exercise of Nazi power.) Once inside, the Reichstag members had to seek passage into the assemblage through a wall of brown-shirted SA troops. (The SA, or *Sturmabteilung*, i.e., "storm detachment," Hitler's early army of storm troopers. Originally organized to protect Nazi meetings and oppose political rivals, the SA, a collection of mostly thugs and brawlers, lost in a power struggle with the SS and was disbanded in 1935.) Unsurprisingly, when Reichstag president Hermann Göring announced the results of the day's voting, the Enabling Bill became law by an affirmative vote of 441 to 94.

Hitler was still not the absolute dictator of Germany, but, in Alan Bullock's words, "he had full power to set aside the Constitution." Moreover, as Bullock so starkly notes, "The street gangs had seized control of the resources of a great modern State, the gutter had come to power."[38]

Gleichschaltung

On March 31, only a week after the passage of the Enabling Law, the central government passed another law called the Temporary Law for Coordination of the States with the Reich. This law initiated the *Gleichschaltung*, or "coordination," process, which formed a vital part of Hitler's early consolidation of power.

The "coordination" law decreed that state parliaments must conform to the new party strength in the Reichstag, that is, state parliaments must include members of the Nazi Party in numbers proportionate to those serving in the Reichstag. Communists were to be excluded. In addition, the law authorized state governments to issue laws in breach of their state constitutions.

"But this solution lasted only a week," recalls William L. Shirer, who goes on to write:

> The Chancellor [Hitler], working at feverish haste, issued a new law on April 7, appointing Reich Governors (*Reichsstaathaelter*) in all the states and empowering them to appoint and remove local governments, dissolve the diets [local legislatures], and appoint and dismiss state officials and judges. Each of the new governors was a Nazi and they were "required" to carry out "the general policy laid down by the Reich Chancellor."

> Thus, within a fortnight of receiving full powers from the Reichstag [through passage of the Enabling Law], Hitler . . . had abolished the separate powers of the historic states and made them subject to the central authority of the Reich, which was in his hands.[39]

The states were the first to fall to the *Gleichschaltung* process, followed in quick succession by rival political parties, the labor force, agriculture, and every remaining facet of German life and culture, until all were "consolidated" under the Nazi regime.

"It [*Gleichschaltung*] appeared to be an efficient process of unifying the nation and was received with little alarm," writes John Toland. "What it did was bring the political, economical and social life of the nation under the control of the NSDAP [Nazis] and plant the seeds of a faceless dictatorship. There was little resistance primarily because Hitler kept within the law."[40]

Hitler's coordination process affected the lives of all Germans, but none so alarmingly as Germany's Jewish population. Holocaust scholars Abraham J. and Hershel Edelheit explain why in their ominous definition of *Gleichschaltung*:

> A *volkish* idea that the national organism is greater than the sum of its individual parts. These must, therefore, be unified into one monolithic whole that will bring about the rise of the Teutonic order and the "messianic" age. Obviously anything not of the *Volk*, i.e., alien elements, must be gotten rid of, as these will act as a cancer destroying the organism. This primarily meant the Jews. The Nazi Final Solution is only the logical outcome of this policy.[41]

And in conjunction with his *Gleichschaltung* program, Hitler framed a series of laws aimed at stripping Jews in Germany of all rights.

Anti-Jewish Boycott

After the Nazis' *Machtergreifung*, or seizure of power, in January 1933, they launched their first assault on German Jewry on the first day of the following April. The assault came in the form of a boycott against Jewish shops, offices, and businesses.

On the night before the boycott, the following item appeared in the official Nazi newspaper *Völkischer Beobachter* (*Racial Observer*) as part of an eleven-part order occupying the entire front page:

> In every local branch and organizational section of the National Socialist German Workers' Party, Action Committees are to be formed immediately for the practical systematic implementation of a boycott of Jewish shops, Jewish goods, Jewish doctors and Jewish lawyers. The Action Committees are responsible for making sure that the boycott will not affect innocent persons, but will hit the guilty all the harder.[42]

The boycott commenced as scheduled on April 1, ostensibly as an act of reprisal against Jewish *Greuelpropaganda* (atrocity propaganda). "For several months terror had been directed against individual Jews, Jewish organizations, and Jewish institutions and businesses as well as other 'enemies of the regime,'" writes Leni Yahil, professor emerita at Haifa University. According to Yahil:

> These activities aroused strong reaction abroad, and there were growing indications that they might affect Germany's foreign relations and exacerbate its economic problems. The Nazi leaders needed a period of domestic tranquility to secure their control of the country; hence, they were eager to put a stop to the uncontrolled terror and the so-called atrocity propaganda it provoked.[43]

The April 1 action began at 10 A.M. sharp throughout the country. "It was designed to show the outside world who the real rulers of Germany were," Yahil explains, "and prove that they were strong enough 'to maintain order.'"[44] In practice, as John Toland tells it:

Brownshirts were posted before the doors of most Jewish stores and offices. There was little violence and the young SA men were, for the most part, polite when reminding shoppers that they were about to patronize a Jewish business. "Little knots of passers-by collected to watch the performance—interested, amused or merely apathetic." [A quotation from Christopher Isherwood, an English-born American novelist who resided in Berlin at that time.] In fact a good number went into the department store Isherwood was watching. He too entered, bought the first thing he saw, a nutmeg grater, and walked out twirling his parcel. This act of defiance was greeted by a wink from one of the young SA monitors. Although the boycotters got support from organizations which called upon farmers to support them, [the boycott] was ineffective against the large department stores and banks and ended after three days.[45]

On April 4 an official declaration informed the nation that the "boycott has achieved its purpose and is over."[46]

Anti-Jewish Legislation

The end of the abbreviated boycott signaled the beginning of what Klaus Fischer calls "the first phase of legalized racism . . . as Nazi Germany was moving steadily toward a policy of legalized expulsion, ghettoization, and extermination of Jews."[47]

Three days later the government enacted three new laws calculated to limit the number of Jews in civil service, in the legal profession, and in the election of assessors, jurors, and commercial judges. Thereafter, an avalanche of new laws, most of them aimed at excluding Jews from the economical, cultural, and social life of Germany, thundered down from the pinnacle of power now occupied by Hitler. The Reichstag passed eight more new restrictive laws in April alone.

Posters urge people not to buy from Jewish shops. Although the boycott was largely ineffective, it foreshadowed more brutal efforts to ostracize the Jews.

A soldier stands beside a placard that reads "Germans! Defend yourselves! Do not buy from Jews!" In addition to the anti-Jewish boycott, the Nazis also passed a series of laws that restricted Jews' involvement in German society.

In the view of Abraham J. and Hershel Edelheit, "the Nazis went through three phases in their anti-Jewish legislation," which they categorize as follows:

First, between April 1933 and September 1935, the Nazis severely limited the sphere of economic activity permitted to German Jews. Second, between September 1935 and 1937, the Nazis defined the racial component of their legislation and reduced Jews to the status of *Reichsangehörigen*—subjects of the state, or something less than second-class citizens. Third, between September 1937 and September 1939, the Nazis completely eliminated German Jews from the economy.

With the outbreak of war and the Nazi occupation of much of Europe, existing legislation was extended and made more systematic. In effect, legislation announced in this period laid the legal precedents for the Final Solution.[48]

In their definitive work *History of the Holocaust*, the Edelheits list and briefly define 201 laws—mainly anti-Semitic—enacted by the Nazi regime between April 1933 and September 1944. They further catalog more than 260 anti-Semitic laws promulgated by Axis states and Nazi-occupied nations within a similar time frame.

Laws, of course, require rigid enforcement if they are to be effective. So it came as no coincidence that Heinrich Himmler was appointed police president of Munich on March 9, 1933.

Police State

Heinrich Himmler, outwardly meek appearing but inwardly blindly ambitious and driven to the pursuit of power, joined the Nazi Party in 1927. After serving in several party posts, including deputy head of the SS, he was appointed to head the elite guard. As *SS-Reichsführer* (SS leader), he quickly demonstrated his keen organizational ability, expanding the SS membership from fewer than three hundred members in 1929 to more than fifty thousand in 1933.

During this time, although the SS was nominally subordinate to the SA, headed by Ernst Röhm, Himmler organized his own secret civilian security organization, the *Sicherheitsdienst*, or SD, under Reinhard Heydrich. The SD would be named as the sole political and counterespionage agency for the Nazi Party in June 1934, and would thereafter play a fearsome part in the destruction of the Jews.

While Himmler was climbing steadily toward the top of the Nazi power structure, Hermann Göring was busily strengthening his number-two position in Hitler's political hierarchy. On April 26, 1933, as part of his ongoing move to gain control of the nation's police, Göring incorporated the political police of Prussia into a new organization called the Gestapo (from *GEheime STAats-POlizei*, or secret state police).

The activities of Göring's Gestapo and Himmler's SD soon overlapped, and the two power aspirants entered into a fierce rivalry. Each wanted to become head of a unified political police force. Himmler gradually took control of the political police in a series of German states and eventually prevailed in his struggle with Göring. In April 1934 the owlish-looking SS chief took over the leadership of the entire unified political police force.

For more than a decade under Himmler and his subordinates, the SS orchestrated the murders of millions of Jews and other alleged enemies of the state. And the Gestapo built an enduring reputation as the most feared

Police president Heinrich Himmler (wearing glasses) reviews Viennese police units. Himmler was in charge of enforcing Germany's anti-Semitic laws.

Something to Cheer About

William L. Shirer, renowned foreign correspondent and chronicler of the twelve-year Nazi reign, was working for the Paris *Herald* when news of Hitler's blood purge of Ernst Röhm and the SA (the Night of the Long Knives) reached the outside world. In his acclaimed *Berlin Diary*, Shirer writes:

PARIS, *June* 30

Berlin was cut off for several hours today, but late this afternoon telephone communication was reestablished. And what a story! Hitler and Göring have purged the S.A., shooting many of its leaders. Röhm, arrested by Hitler himself, was allowed to commit suicide in a Munich jail, according to one agency report. The French are pleased. They think this is the beginning of the end for the Nazis. Wish I could get a post in Berlin. It's a story I'd like to cover.

In a follow-up entry about the purge two weeks later, Shirer reports:

PARIS, *July* 14

It now develops that Hitler's purge was more drastic than first reported. Röhm did not kill himself, but was shot on the orders of Hitler. Other dead: [Edmund] Heines, notorious Nazi boss of Silesia, Dr. Erich Klausner, leader of the "Catholic Action" [spiritual revival advocates] in Germany, Fritz von Bose and Edgar Jung, two of [then Vice Chancellor Franz von] Papen's secretaries, (Papen himself narrowly escaped with his life), Gregor Strasser, who used to be second in importance to Hitler in the Nazi Party, and [former chancellor] General [Kurt] von Schleicher and his wife, the latter two murdered in cold blood. I see [Gustav] von Kahr is on the list, the man who balked Hitler's Beer House *Putsch* in 1923. Hitler has thus taken his personal revenge. Yesterday, on Friday the 13th, Hitler got away with his explanation in the Reichstag. When he screamed: "The supreme court of the German people during these twenty-four hours consisted of myself!" the deputies [Reichstag members] rose and cheered. One had almost forgotten how strong sadism and masochism are in the German people.

secret police organization ever to impose itself on humankind. Together, the SS and its Gestapo component held Germany and much of Europe captive in torment and terror; together, they carved a swath of human misery unequaled in time, while establishing the end-all definition of a police state.

Promises to Keep

On October 14, 1933, Hitler took to the airwaves and announced to the world that Germany was withdrawing from the League of Nations. In his radio address, he said: "To be written down as a member of such an institution possessing no such equality of rights is, for an honor-loving nation of sixty-five million folk and for a government which loves honor, an intolerable humiliation."[49]

This action represented Hitler's symbolic rejection of the Versailles treaty, which, in the eyes of many observers, unfairly punished Germany for losing World War I. It also served notice to the world that Hitler was a new force to be reckoned with. And it paved the way for Germany's rearmament.

By the end of June 1934, only one obstacle remained to bar Hitler's path to an absolute dictatorship: the increasingly unruly element of radicals concentrated in Captain Ernst Röhm's SA. To Hitler's embarrassment, and to the ire of his military and industrialist supporters, Röhm and his Brownshirts persisted in calling for a "continuing revolution."[50] Hitler removed the source of his embarrassment with characteristic ruthlessness.

Rallying the support of party and army leaders, particularly Heinrich Himmler's SS, Hitler staged a blood purge on the night of June 29–30, 1934. Hitler and Himmler both personally participated in the purge that became popularly known as the Night of the Long Knives (*Die Nacht der langen Messer*). During the purge, at least seventy-seven top Nazis, including Röhm, and about a hundred others were killed.

Barely more than a month later, Reich president Paul von Hindenburg died on August 2, whereupon Hitler immediately abolished the title of president and declared himself führer and Reich chancellor of the German state. To ensure the allegiance of the armed forces, he then required all officers and men to swear an oath—not to the nation but to himself:

I swear by God this sacred oath, that I will render unconditional obedience to Adolf Hitler, the Führer of the German Reich and people, Supreme Comman-

Hitler gives the Nazi salute to his troops as Ernst Röhm stands beside him. When Röhm continued to be an unruly element in Hitler's plans, Hitler had him killed.

der of the Armed Forces, and will be ready as a brave soldier to risk my life at any time for this oath.[51]

"Later and often," writes William L. Shirer, "by honoring their oath they dishonored themselves as human beings and trod in the mud the moral code of their corps."[52] And millions died because they did.

Hitler had traveled far from the gutters of Vienna. At the age of only forty-five, he now stood undisputed and unchallenged as Germany's dictator—and free to keep the promises that he made in the pages of *Mein Kampf.*

The Doom of Jewish Life in Germany

In September 1934 at Nuremberg, the new führer proclaimed that the revolution was over. "This revolution has achieved without exception all that was expected of it," he declared. "In the next thousand years there will be no new revolution."[53]

The Thousand-Year Reich was born. And the Nazis' wholesale persecution of the Jews began.

The Nuremberg Laws of 1935

Hitler came to power pledging to create a Germany in which Jews were set apart from their fellow Germans and denied their place as vital, functioning members of German society. To clear the way for his all-out assault against the Jews, Hitler took steps to legally define Jewish citizenship and what constituted Jewishness.

On September 15, 1935, at a special session of the Reichstag held during a party rally in Nuremberg, Hitler decreed two laws for this purpose: the *Reichsbürgergesetz* (State Citizenship Law), and the *Gesetz zum Schutze des deutschen Blutes und der deutschen Ehre* (Law for the Protection of German Blood and German Honor). The first law effectively stripped German Jews of their citizenship by declaring them to be subjects of the German state; while the second law defined who was a Jew, who was an Aryan

(Nordic), and who was a *Mischling* (part Jew). All subsequent anti-Semitic legislation invoked in Nazi Germany and throughout Europe during World War II owed its existence in some measure to the tenets of hate crafted into these two laws.

Hitler himself, while introducing the laws to the Reichstag at Nuremberg, hinted at an impending change of Nazi policy toward the Jews. He described the Law for the Protection of German Blood and Honor as "an attempt to regulate by law a problem that, in the event of repeated failure, would have to be transferred by law to the National Socialist Party for final solution."[54]

During the next four years, the Nazi regime promulgated at least 121 additional laws, decrees, and ordinances designed to systematically reduce the status of Jews in Germany to that of undesirable nonentities. These statutes rendered it impossible for Jews to sustain their life in the Third Reich.

The Executioner's Sword

Following the enactment of the Nuremberg Laws of 1935, Hitler began implementing the second (persecution) phase of his goal to rid Germany (and later all of Europe) of Jews. And he laid the groundwork for extending Germany's borders—in accordance with his doctrine of lebensraum (living space)—to make room for an expanding German population. The implementation of lebensraum included the removal of Jews (one way or another) from living spaces allocated by the Nazis for the sole use of German citizens.

That in turn would set the third (expulsion) phase of *Die Endlösung* in motion, commencing with the mass exodus of approximately half of Germany's half-million Jews. The Jews were allowed—even encouraged—by the Nazis to emigrate from 1933 until the outbreak of the war in 1939. At the same time, the Nazis—spearheaded by Himmler's SS—commenced purging hundreds of municipalities to make them *Judenrein* (free of Jews), forcing the Jews to take refuge in larger towns and cities within Germany.

Hatred for the Jew became the dominant theme of SS doctrine. According to Lucy S. Dawidowicz:

In 1936 a standard lecture for SS units contained the following passage: "A Jew is a parasite. Wherever he flourishes, the people die. . . . Elimination of the Jew from our community is to be regarded as an emergency defense measure." The "right of emergency defense" was the title Hitler used for the last chapter of *Mein Kampf*, in which he had advocated the gassing of "twelve or fifteen thousand" Jews. The SS text reveals the emerging role of the SS as an expression of Hitler's will and as the central executing arm in the Final Solution of the Jewish Question.[55]

On June 17, 1936, Hitler named Heinrich Himmler chief of all German police. Himmler, already *SS-Reichsführer* and deputy chief of the Gestapo (under Hermann Göring), now controlled all uniformed and criminal police in Germany and reported to only the führer himself.

By now Himmler had come to regard the Jew as an ideological enemy as well as an enemy of the state. He perceived his role and that of the SS as follows:

We shall unremittingly fulfill our task, to be the guarantors of the internal security

A Jewish family loads their furniture and other possessions onto a horse-drawn cart as crowds gather to watch and jeer. Jews were moved out of areas that were deemed "German only" by Hitler.

Jews are searched and arrested on a Berlin street. Due to Hitler's plan to eventually eliminate the Jews, those that remained in Germany were harassed at every opportunity.

of Germany, just as the Wehrmacht [German army] guarantees the safety of the honor, the greatness, and the peace of the Reich from the outside. We shall take care that never more in Germany, the heart of Europe, can the Jewish-Bolshevistic revolution of subhumans be kindled internally or by emissaries from abroad [that is, by elements of international Jewry or Communists]. Pitilessly we shall be a merciless executioner's sword for all these forces whose existence and doings we know . . . whether it be today, or in decades, or in centuries.[56]

While Germans exchanged whispered rumors of an impending external war, the SS wielded its sword in an internal war against Germany's ideological enemies—most particularly the Jews.

Hitler's Four-Year Plan

On September 9, 1936, at the annual Nazi Party rally held in Nuremberg, Hitler introduced a Four-Year Plan for revitalizing Germany's economy. In a proclamation, he stated:

In four years Germany must be wholly independent of foreign areas in those materials which can be produced in any way through German ability, through our chemical and machine industry, as well as through our mining industry. The re-building of this great German raw material industry will serve to give employment to the masses. . . . But in addition, Germany cannot relinquish the solution of its colonial demands. The right of the German people to live is surely as great as that of other nations.[57]

Hitler's proclamation was significant for at least two reasons: First, attaining self-sufficiency in raw materials embodied an essential element of German rearmament; and second, Hitler's reference to "the solution of its colonial demands" represented another brick in the road to German expansionism (and thus war) in pursuit of lebensraum.

Hitler entrusted the implementation of his Four-Year Plan to Hermann Göring, an amateur in economic affairs. The plan was later continued into the war years, during which time Göring was again and again compelled to use forced labor to keep the plan in operation. Ultimately, millions of workers from Nazi-occupied countries—many of them Jews—were deported to Germany and forced to work in support of the German war effort. Toward the end of 1944, the life expectancy of such laborers averaged no more than a few months. Hundreds of thousands died in German labor camps.

The Hossbach Memorandum

On November 5, 1937, Hitler convened a meeting with his military chiefs, his Wehrmacht adjutant, Colonel Friedrich Hossbach, and Foreign Minister Constantin von Neurath in the Reich chancellery. Hitler, as noted by Colonel Hossbach, first swore them all to secrecy. He then request-

ed "in the interest of a long-term German policy, that his exposition be regarded, in the event of his death, as his last will and testament."[58] He went on to outline his policy: "The aim of German policy was to make secure and to preserve the racial community and to enlarge it. It was therefore a question of space [lebensraum]."[59] He told his startled audience that Germany's problems (not the least of which was the Jewish question) could only be resolved by the use of force. Germany could not survive without expanding its living space in Europe, he said. War must be risked to attain that goal.

Hitler appointed Hermann Göring to lead his plan to reindustrialize Germany. The plan would eventually involve the implementation of forced labor camps, where hundreds of thousands of slave laborers would die.

Screams of Blood Lust

In a speech made to three thousand members of the Nazi elite in April 1937, Hitler once again revealed his anti-Semitism. "After giving practical advice on a variety of subjects," writes John Toland in his biography *Adolf Hitler*, "he abruptly turned to the Jewish menace, talking in the private, obscure terms everyone in the hall understood." Toland quotes Hitler as saying:

> The question to me is never to take a step that might have to be retracted and bring harm to us. You know, I always go to the very brink of boldness but not beyond. . . . I am not going to challenge my opponent immediately to a fight. I don't say, "Fight," just for the pleasure of fighting. Instead I say, "I will destroy you."

"His last words, leaving no doubt that he meant to solve the problem by killing the Jews," Toland concludes, "were drowned out by a spontaneous mass scream of blood lust. This flesh-creeping roar was preserved on tape, a reminder of man's primal brutality and how like the shrieks of the mob in the Roman Colosseum for the death of a fallen gladiator it must have been!"

Whether one chooses to believe that Hitler planned the Final Solution from the beginning, or that his decision to annihilate the Jews gradually evolved over the years, one thing is certain: An undertaking of such enormity could best be undertaken within the sealed borders of a nation at war. And war, as he would reveal at the Hossbach conference, was precisely what Hitler had in mind.

It was now a question of how to gain the most at the lowest cost. He described three scenarios of resistance that might result from their aggression.

Of particular advantage, he emphasized, would be the "annexation of Czechoslovakia and Austria," which would afford Germany better strategic borders, additional foodstuffs for some six million Germans in the Reich, and enough manpower for twelve new army divisions. No matter what course of action is decided upon, he told them, Germany must strike while at the peak of its military power, which he estimated as no later than 1943–1945. And he warned that Britain, France, and Russia must be considered as "power factors in our political calculations."[60]

The formalized minutes of that meeting became known as the Hossbach Memorandum. It was later regarded by the War Crimes Tribunal at Nuremberg in 1945–1946 as the first evidence of Hitler's aggressive intentions. But Klaus P. Fischer, one of the more recent historians of Germany's Nazi era, maintains, "Far too much importance has been attributed to this document by the prosecution at Nuremberg and by later historians searching for a 'smoking gun.'" Fischer believes:

> The conference was not the catalyst for Hitler's war of aggression; it was simply Hitler's means of clearing the air and testing the waters with his military chiefs. Judging by their cautious, if not downright alarmed, responses, Hitler knew that he had to shake up his high command in order to get the sort of generals who would obediently do his bidding as his "mad dogs."[61]

Hitler did in fact shake up his top military commanders. But it should also be noted that

German troops marched into Austria on March 12, 1938—only five months after the Hossbach conference—and Germany's annexation of Austria was completed the next day. A similar fate befell Czechoslovakia a year and three days later on March 15, 1939. And with Germany's acquisition of these bordering territories, the number of Jews under Nazi rule increased by about a half million.

"Extraordinary Satisfaction"

As the gray-clad soldiers of Hitler's Wehrmacht marched out of Germany and down the road to war, Himmler's black-uniformed SS troops and civilian Gestapo agents were diligently conducting a well-ordered campaign designed to purge the Third Reich of Jews and Jewish influence. From 1933 until the outbreak of war in 1939, although Jews were driven from public life by the Nazi regime and forced to endure ongoing abuse and denigration, fewer than a hundred Jews were included among several thousand alleged enemies of the state murdered in concentration camps at Buchenwald, Sachsenhausen, and Dachau.

By 1938, encouraged by official Nazi policy, more than half of Germany's half-million Jewish citizens had emigrated, leaving behind shops, homes, possessions, livelihoods, friends, and even family members. Those Jews who, for whatever reason,

Lieutenant Adolf Eichmann was in charge of the forced emigration of the Jews from Germany. Largely responsible for the genocide of millions of Jews, Eichmann said that the idea brought him "extraordinary satisfaction."

either could not or would not leave Germany were targeted for increasing acts of physical violence at the hands of SS thugs and others.

In March 1938 Lieutenant (*Untersturmführer*) Adolf Eichmann, a self-educated authority in Jewish affairs, was afforded his first opportunity to apply his expertise. Journalist Hannah Arendt, who would later gain renown covering Eichmann's postwar trial in Israel, describes his new assignment in these terms:

> After the *Anschluss* (the incorporation of Austria into the Reich) . . . he was sent to Vienna to organize a kind of emigra-

tion that had been utterly unknown in Germany, where up to the fall of 1938 the fiction was maintained that Jews if they so desired were permitted, but were not forced, to leave the country. . . .

> But what happened in Vienna in March, 1938, was altogether different. Eichmann's task had been defined as "forced emigration," and the words meant exactly what they said: all Jews, regardless of their desires and regardless of their citizenship, were forced to emigrate—an act which in ordinary language is called expulsion.[62]

In under eighteen months, Eichmann oversaw the "forced emigration" of some 150,000 Jews. But this represented only a trickle in the torrent of Jewish expulsions to follow from all over Europe.

The new director of Jewish emigration in Vienna (and later in Prague and elsewhere) was the same Adolf Eichmann who would, during the war's last days, tell his men: "I will jump into my grave laughing, because the fact that I have the death of five million Jews [or 'enemies of the Reich,' as he always claimed to have said] on my conscience gives me extraordinary satisfaction."[63] As 1938 drew to a close, the inevitable doom of Jewish life under the Third Reich became clear and was assured by men like Eichmann.

Night of the Broken Glass

On October 28, 1938, the Gestapo, serving in the role of "Alien Police," rounded up between 17,000 and 18,000 Polish Jews, transported them in sealed railway cars to the Polish border, and dumped them into the gray uncertainty of homelessness. Less than a fortnight later, the Nazis' maltreatment of Polish Jews triggered a violent incident at the

German embassy in Paris. The event described in the following paragraphs—based on an earlier account by authors Anthony Read and David Fisher—cleared the way for undisguised Nazi violence against the Jews:

At exactly 8:35 on the unseasonably mild morning of November 7, 1938, a small, dark-haired young man wearing a khaki-colored raincoat arrived outside *À La Fine Lame* ("At the Sharp Blade"), a sporting goods shop at 61, rue du Faubourg Saint-Martin, Paris. The youth approached Mme. Carpe, wife of the shop's owner, as she rolled up the shop's heavy iron security shutters.

"I want to buy a revolver," he told her.

She referred him to her husband, a gunsmith, inside the shop. The young man entered and repeated his request to the owner. M. Carpe, a small, squat, mustached man in his middle years, examined the youth with an eye for details. "Why do you need a revolver?" he asked.

The youth explained that he often carried large sums of money to the bank for

SS guards stop a Jewish man on the streets of Vienna in March 1938. After invading Austria, the Nazis forced all Jews to emigrate from Vienna.

"Our Suffering Was Great"

The forcible deportation of Polish Jews from Germany commenced at the end of October 1938. Zindel Grynszpan, was among those expelled from Hanover, Germany, along with his wife, daughter, and youngest son. Zindel Grynszpan's recollection of the event appears in Martin Gilbert's *The Holocaust: A History of the Jews in Europe During the Second World War* as follows:

> On the 27th October 1938—it was Thursday night at eight o'clock—a policeman came and told us to come to Region II. He said, "You are going to come back immediately; you shouldn't take anything with you. Take with you your passports."

> When I reached the Region, I saw a large number of people; some people were sitting, some standing. People were crying; they [the Nazis] were shouting, "Sign, sign, sign." I had to sign, as all of them did. One of us did not, and his name, I believe, was Gershon Silber, and he had to stand in the corner for twenty-four hours.

> They took us to the concert hall on the banks of the Leine and there, there were people from all areas, about six hundred people. There we stayed until Friday night; about twenty-four hours; then they took us in police trucks, in prisoners' lorries, about twenty men in each truck, and they took us to the railway station. The streets were black with people shouting, "The Jews out to Palestine."

> After that, when we got to the train, they took us by train to Neubenschen on the German-Polish border. It was Shabbat morning; Saturday morning. When we reached Neubenschen at 6 A.M. there came trains from all sorts of places, Leipzig, Cologne, Dusseldorf, Essen, Bielefeld, Bremen. Together we were about twelve thousand people. . . .

> The SS were giving us, as it were, protective custody, and we walked two kilometers [1.24 miles] on foot to the Polish border. They told us to go—the SS men were whipping us, those who lingered they hit, and blood was flowing on the road. They tore away their little baggage from them, they treated us in a most barbaric fashion—this was the first time that I'd ever seen the wild barbarism of the Germans.

> They shouted at us: "Run! Run!" I myself received a blow and I fell in a ditch. My son helped me, and he said, "Run, run, dad—otherwise you'll die!" When we got to the open border—we reached what was called the green border, the Polish border—first of all, the women went in.

> Then a Polish general and some officers arrived, and they examined the papers and saw that we were Polish citizens, that we had special passports. It was decided to let us enter Poland.

"Zindel Grynszpan [after arriving in the frontier town of Zbaszyn] decided to send a postcard to his [oldest] son Hirsch [Herschel], in Paris, describing his family's travails," adds Martin Gilbert. "The young man, enraged by what he read, went to the German Embassy in Paris, and on 6 November 1938 [most sources record the date as 7 November], shot the first German official who received him, Ernst vom Rath."

his father and said, "I want to be able to protect myself."

M. Carpe eyed him carefully—a slight young man of only about five feet two inches in height and a weight barely in excess of a hundred pounds—and saw no reason to deny his request. He sold the frail-looking youth a 6.35mm five-shot "hammerless" revolver for 210 francs plus 25 francs for a box of twenty-five cartridges. The gunsmith demonstrated how to load and unload the weapon and how to ready the trigger mechanism for firing.

He then requested the youth's name and address and proper identification in accordance with the law. The young man produced a Polish passport that identified him as Herschel Grynszpan, a name that was to appear on the front pages of newspapers all over the world the next day.

The youth left with his new purchase and rode the *métro* (subway) to the Solferino station, from whence he proceeded on foot to an elegant four-story mansion at number 78, rue de Lille. High above a central entrance surmounted by two stone eagles, the scarlet, white, and swastika flag of the Third Reich hung limply in the morning stillness.

Herschel Grynszpan entered the German embassy for the first time shortly after 9:30 A.M. In an incredible lapse of security, the benign-looking youth, under the guise of having an important document to deliver, was directed to the office of Ernst vom Rath, a third secretary at the embassy. The twenty-nine-year-old vom Rath, tall, fair-haired, and earnest of face, admitted Grynszpan to his office and asked to see the document.

Young Grynszpan reached into the inside pocket of his coat and screamed, "You are a *sale boche* [filthy kraut] and here, in the name of twelve thousand persecuted Jews, is your document." The innocent-appearing youth then emptied his 6.35mm revolver into the body of the incredulous diplomat.

Grynszpan surrendered himself immediately after the shooting to French policeman François Autret, who led the young avenger on foot to the police station at 2, rue de Bourgogne, fewer than five hundred meters (547 yards) from the embassy. The mortally wounded vom Rath died two days later, passing into Nazi martyrdom at 4:25 P.M.[64]

On November 7, 1938, seventeen-year-old Herschel Grynszpan (pictured) entered the German embassy in Paris and killed German diplomat Ernst vom Rath. Grynszpan's action was in retaliation for the forced deportation of his Polish-Jewish parents.

On the night of vom Rath's death—November 9–10, 1938—the Nazis answered violence with violence, conducting a pogrom against the Jews throughout Germany, Austria, and the Sudetenland (an area of Bohemia). The Nazis tried to characterize their actions as a spontaneous popular response to vom Rath's assassination by a Jew. In reality, they had preplanned the event in anticipation of some small excuse to begin an assault on Jews and their establishments. A confidential report issued the next day by Reinhard Heydrich, now head of the Reich Central Security Office (*Reichssicherheithsauptant*, or RSHA), stated:

The extent of the destruction of Jewish shops and houses cannot yet be verified by figures. . . . 815 shops destroyed, 171 dwellings set on fire or destroyed only indicate a fraction of the actual damage so far as arson is concerned. . . . 119 synagogues were set on fire, and another 76 completely destroyed. . . . 20,000 Jews were arrested. 36 deaths were reported and those seriously injured were also numbered at 36. Those killed and injured are Jews.[65]

Commenting on the report, William L. Shirer adds: "The ultimate number of murders of Jews that night is believed to have been several times the preliminary figure. Heydrich himself a day after the preliminary report gave the number of Jewish shops looted as 7,500."[66] The pillage lasted for fifteen hours,

Broken glass from looted Jewish shops gives evidence to Kristallnacht, *when the Nazis violently destroyed Jewish property and murdered and arrested Jewish citizens following the assassination of vom Rath.*

leaving the streets of German cities littered with broken glass. Hence the event entered into history under the name of *Kristallnacht*—also called Night of the Broken Glass. Herschel Grynszpan, while in Nazi custody, disappeared sometime in the early 1940s.

Worse Days Ahead

During the next six months, as many as a thousand more Jews were slain. On January 30, 1939, Hitler, addressing the Reichstag on the sixth anniversary of his accession to power, delivered a clear warning to the Jews of Europe:

> If international finance Jewry within Europe and abroad should succeed once more in plunging the peoples into a world war, then the consequence will not be the Bolshevization [Communization] of the world and therewith a victory of Jewry, but on the contrary, the destruction of the Jewish race in Europe.[67]

Since the Hossbach Memorandum had already made clear Hitler's plan for aggressive expansion, this statement constituted a declaration of war against the Jews.

As many historians have noted, no one knows with certainty when—or even whether—Hitler gave the order to annihilate the Jews. No written document has ever been found. It is generally surmised that Hitler may have feared adverse public reaction, coupled with a compulsion for secrecy, and perhaps a psychological need to distance himself from the atrocities. Accordingly, he revealed his role in the killing process only to a few trusted underlings, such as Himmler, Goebbels, Bormann, and Göring.

"But the fact is that Hitler had been step-by-step the guiding spirit of what happened to the Jews since he gained power in

Although no document has ever been found to fully implicate Hitler in the plan to annihilate the Jews, historians have pieced together a trail of more subtle clues that lay the blame on his shoulders.

1933," writes Klaus P. Fischer. Continuing, he asserts:

> From the very beginning the machinery for the implementation of the war on the Jews was effected through a chain of command that began with Hitler, moved to Himmler, to Heydrich's Reich Main Security Office, to Section IV of the SD (Gestapo Müller), to Section IV-B-4 (Eichmann and Jewish affairs), and finally to the *Einsatzgruppen* and Death-Head's Units in the concentration camps.[68]

The Doom of Jewish Life in Germany 49

The Euthanasia Program

On July 14, 1933, the Nazis enacted the Law for the Protection of Hereditary Health. Its purpose was to implement eugenic measures designed to improve the quality of the German race. This ushered in a development that led to the enforced "mercy" killings of the incurably insane and to the extermination of peoples considered to be biologically inferior, such as Jews, Slavs, and Gypsies.

In *The Holocaust: The Fate of European Jewry*, historian Leni Yahil describes what is known today as the Nazis' Euthanasia Program:

The operation was carried out in five stages. First the candidates were selected from among the inmates of the institutions; next they were taken to a transit center from which they were transported to the nearest "euthanasia" installation [at one of six locations: Grafeneck, Hartheim, Brandenburg, Sonnenstein, Bernburg, and Hadamar]. There they underwent a perfunctory medical test and were sent, in batches of twenty to thirty, to a sealed room into which carbon monoxide was pumped. Finally the bodies were removed and burned in an attached crematorium, but not before all gold teeth had been extracted and some of their brains had been excised for purposes of "scientific research." The first experiments were conducted in January 1940; by August of the following year 70,273 people had been exterminated in . . . installations set up for *Sonderbehandlung* (special treatment). This particular term from the Nazi language of concealment continued to be used when referring to killing by gas, even when it was later conducted in death camps with no medical connotations. . . .

Hitler's assumption that in wartime it would be easier and more simple to implement this scheme was refuted by the great number of people who became aware of what was being perpetrated in the special "curative institutions." Leaders of the Catholic and Protestant churches protested to government ministries and some, including several bishops, even raised their voices in public protest. Dr. [Antonius] Hilfrich, bishop of Limburg an der Lahn near Hadamar, where one of the main installations was located, wrote on August 13, 1941, to the minister of justice with a copy to the minister of the interior and the minister of church affairs. He noted that attempts had been made to silence public outcry by means of threats but that the illegal activities had not been halted. The local children, he wrote, now recognized the buses with blacked-out windows in which the victims were transported and pointed them out, "Look, there's the murder-box coming again" or slandered one another, "You're crazy. They'll take you to the oven at Hadamar."

Hitler, apparently persuaded by continued public outcry and increasing court actions taken against participating doctors by relatives of the victims, decided to discontinue the organized action. He halted the Euthanasia Program on August 24, 1941.

During the summer of 1939, Hitler authorized the organization of a euthanasia program—code name *Aktion T4*—for the methodical killing of mentally and physically handicapped children and adults. Many of the selected patients were murdered in gas chambers disguised as shower rooms; others were killed in mobile vans into which carbon monoxide was pumped. By August 1941, when Hitler ordered the program terminated, 70,273 people had been "disinfected"[69] (gassed to death) and thousands more shot by SS units. *Aktion T4* served as a harbinger of a far greater evil to follow.

Hitler unleashed the machinery of mass destruction on September 1, 1939, sending German troops across Germany's eastern border into Poland. Hitler's aggressive action extended his expansionist policy of lebensraum, signaled the start of World War II, and ended all semblance of tolerable Jewish life in Germany. And worse days ahead loomed large for the Jews of Europe.

CHAPTER 4

Slow Death

The third time period of Hitler's commitment to rid Europe of all Jews commenced simultaneously with his eastward move, that is, with the invasion of Poland on

German troops invade Poland on September 1, 1939. An additional 2 million Jews came under German rule after the invasion.

September 1, 1939. Up to then, the Nazis had conceived and carried out two purported "solutions" to the "Jewish question" with limited success.

Their first solution was the expulsion of Jews from hundreds of villages and small towns throughout Germany, in which many had lived and worked all their lives. Thousands of Jewish families, some with roots that reached back for a millennium or more, were forced to move to larger municipalities inside Germany. This was done both to encourage Jews to leave Germany, as well as to make rural living space available for the resettlement of German *Volk* (literally, "people"; in this sense, racially pure German citizens).

Their second solution—emigration—caused roughly half of Germany's 550,000 Jews to relocate, mainly to the United States (100,000), Argentina (63,000), the United Kingdom (52,000), and Palestine (33,000). But even this substantial reduction in the Jewish population during the third (expulsion) phase of the Final Solution failed to solve the so-called problem. The need for a third solution became clear to the Germans when they invaded Poland and two million more Jews came under their rule.

During the first two months of the war, the Nazis murdered more than ten thousand civilians in the streets of Poland, including some three thousand Jews—a slaughter unprecedented in twentieth-century Europe. According to Lucy S. Dawidowicz:

> Within a few months of the German occupation, thousands of Jewish settlements were erased from the map of Poland, their inhabitants ejected without notice, forbidden to take bare necessities, condemned to exposure, hunger, and homelessness. . . . Some 330,000 Jews—one-tenth of the Jews in Poland—became homeless refugees, beggars of bread and shelter, candidates for disease. . . .
>
> Terror enveloped the Jews. The Germans reenacted the Kristallnacht in every town and city they invaded and occupied. All over Poland synagogues went up in flames. (Those spared the fire were desecrated, turned into stables, garages, and public latrines.) Everywhere Germans organized pogroms, rounding up the non-Jewish population to witness and learn how to mock, abuse, injure, and murder Jews. Unbridled killing and senseless violence became daily commonplaces for the Jews; the fear of sudden death became normal and habitual.[70]

Although Poland's Jews constituted by far the largest Jewish population within the expanding borders of Germany's Third Reich, no immediate plans existed for dealing with them. During the winter of 1939–1940, however, a plan emerged. (It seems worth mentioning here that the Germans' apparent step-by-step, trial-and-error approach to controlling the Jewish population tends to enhance the functionalists' contention that the Final Solution *evolved*.)

Ghettoization

In the spring of 1940, the Nazis embarked on a third solution to the Jewish question—*ghettoization*. The medieval concept of the ghetto—a confined area within a city or state in which Jews were made to live because of social or economic discrimination—was revived. Tens of thousands of Polish Jews were driven from their homes and forced to live in restricted areas.

The term *ghetto* (but not the concept) originated in Venice from the name of the closed Jewish quarter—*Gheto Nuovo*, or New Foundry—established in 1516. To segregate, isolate, and more effectively control the massive number of Jews within their expanding domain, the Nazis revived the

This photo of Warsaw, Poland, shows the tall fences topped with barbed wire that were used to keep the Jews within the ghetto.

ghetto concept, first in Poland, and then elsewhere in Europe. Holocaust authorities Abraham J. and Hershel Edelheit define the origin and scope of the Nazi-established ghetto like this:

On September 21, 1939, RSHA chief Reinhard Heydrich penned orders for the civil authorities in the General Government [official name for Nazi-occupied Poland] to establish ghettos and Judenräte [Jewish councils serving as buffering agents for Nazi demands upon the Jewish general population], pending the *Gesamtlösung* (total solution) to the Jewish question. The Nazis established a total of 356 ghettos in Poland, the Soviet Union, the Baltic Republics, Romania, and Hungary between 1939 and 1945.

There was no uniform pattern in the establishment, method of isolation, or internal regimes of the ghettos. Indeed, two divergent forms of ghettos existed: closed ghettos, those sealed off by walls, or other physical means, and open ghettos, those that were not sealed off. Generally speaking, open ghettos were located in small towns, where Jews already lived in close proximity to one another and where it was uneconomical to make those who did not so reside move. Open ghettos were often only temporary measures, with the residents being moved to larger ghettos or being sent directly to their deaths.

Closed ghettos, in contrast, were almost always located in larger communities and implied the transfer of all the Jews to a small—usually rundown—neighborhood.[71]

In addition to segregating, isolating, and controlling the Jews, the use of ghettos served the Germans in two other important ways: The more able-bodied among the ghetto dwellers provided a standing source of forced labor; and the ghettos could be cut off to allow for the slow process of starvation to further diminish the Jewish population.

Poland's two largest ghettos were located in Warsaw and Lodz. They confined some 500,000 and 205,000 Jews, respectively, and thus earned dubious claim to surrendering the greatest number of Jews to both sudden and slow death.

Closing the Ring

Warsaw, the capital city of Poland, spans the Vistula River, with two-thirds of the city situated on the west bank and one-third on the east bank. Prior to World War II, the center of Jewish life and culture resided in Warsaw. Its Jewish population of more than 350,000 represented the largest Jewish community in prewar Europe, and second to New York City as the largest in the world.

Poland's cities came under heavy air and artillery attacks as soon as the war broke out. Writes Lucy L. Dawidowicz:

Jews suffered along with everyone else, sharing in the devastation of Polish cities. Warsaw underwent the most massive destruction, as torrents of bombs turned the city into a mass of craters, ruins, and ashes. On September 16, the eve of Rosh Hashana, the Jewish New Year, German planes bombed the dense Jewish quarter, flying so low there could be no mistaking the deliberate intent.

When Warsaw came under siege, the Germans exploded some ten to thirty thousand shells daily on the city. . . .

Some 20,000 Jews lost their lives during the invasion and bombardments; Jewish homes, stores, buildings, workshops, factories, and other installations were destroyed, the losses estimated at 50,000 to 100,000 units. In Warsaw alone, about one-third of Jewish-owned buildings were demolished and the main centers of Jewish trade were reduced to rubble.[72]

Warsaw surrendered to the Germans on September 28. German troops occupied the city the next day.

On October 12, 1939, Hitler appointed party-faithful Hans Frank chief civilian officer for occupied Polish territory and subsequently governor-general of occupied Poland. Frank described his intended governing policy with candor: "Poland shall be treated like a colony: the Poles will become the slaves of the Greater German Empire."[73] His message to the Jews under his rule, delivered in a notorious speech fourteen months later, exceeded his earlier candor:

I ask nothing of the Jews except that they should disappear. They will have to go.... We must destroy the Jews wherever we meet them and whenever opportunity offers so that we can maintain the whole

German troops march into Warsaw, torn asunder by German bombs. Warsaw surrendered on September 28, 1939.

Hitler appointed Hans Frank to govern occupied Poland. Frank's plan was to rule Poland like a colony. In his words, he wanted the Poles to "become the slaves of the Greater German Empire."

introduced similar methods for identifying Jews throughout their conquered territories.) Five days later, he ordered the formation of a *Judenrät* (Jewish council) in each city. By decree, the *Judenrät* was obliged to take orders from the Germans and was held responsible for the efficient execution of the orders; in turn, all Jews in the community were ordered to comply with directives issued by the *Judenrät* to implement German orders. The Germans hoped to soften Jewish resistance to their orders by using the *Judenrät* to buffer themselves from direct contact with the Jewish community.

Although the Gestapo ordered the *Judenrät* on November 4 to form a ghetto in Warsaw within three days, then, for no known reason, rescinded the order, barbed wire had enclosed the populous Jewish quarter as early as October. Two months later the Germans ordered the *Judenrät* to erect wooden signs warning DANGER: EPIDEMIC ZONE at thirty-four street corners leading into the core of the Jewish community. In May 1940 the Germans walled off these accesses, further restricting movement between the Jewish quarter—now a ghetto in all but name—and the rest of the city. Slowly, but ever so surely, the Germans closed the ring around the Jews of Warsaw.

The Warsaw Ghetto

The Germans had begun forming ghettos elsewhere in occupied Poland in October 1939, establishing the first in the town of Piotrków Trybunalski. The first large ghetto was sectioned off in Lodz, a major city in western Poland, in February 1940.

On October 12, 1940, the Germans at last issued a decree ordering the establishment of a ghetto in Warsaw. The edict condemned the Jews—about 30 percent of the city's population—to live in a walled-off

structure of the Reich here. . . . We can't shoot these 3.5 million Jews, but we can take steps which, one way or another, will lead to extermination, in conjunction with the large-scale measures under discussion in the Reich.[74]

Frank began at once to tighten German control over the Jews within the General Government (*Generalgouvernement*), the German name for occupied Poland.

On November 23, 1939, he ordered all Jews over the age of ten to wear white bands with the Star of David on the right arms of both their inner and outer clothing to identify themselves as Jews. (The Nazis later section of Warsaw that represented only 2.4 percent of the city's total area. Guarded walls more than ten feet high and topped with barbed wire, along with a penalty of death for leaving the ghetto confines, kept all but the bravest or most foolhardy Jews inside.

Most of Warsaw's Jews accepted their misfortune with typical Jewish determination, not only to endure but to prevail in the war being waged against them by the Germans. As Leni Yahil comments:

The Jews did not capitulate and did not despair. Instead, they mounted their own war: a war for survival.

Schooled in suffering for centuries, the Jews of Poland were well versed in the ways of the difficult and often desperate struggle for survival. Victims there had always been, but one way or another the Jewish people had always overcome their trials. The crowded conditions in which they lived actually gave them a sense of security and enabled them to carry on the active intellectual life for which they were renown. The impact of this tradition was evident in their behavior during the first phase of the war and the occupation. Deep in their hearts they carried the belief that they would prevail this time as well.[75]

But to prevail in this struggle they would need to overcome cold, hunger, filth, disease, countless deprivations, and a daily diet of German brutalities. The Jews faced this latest challenge armed only with their will to live, faith in God, ingenuity, solidarity of family, sense of community, and even, for many, humor.

Even in their darkest hours, the Jews never lost their sense of humor. When the Germans began suffering military setbacks in Russia in late 1941, anti-German jokes circulated around the ghetto and helped to lift spirits:

"What's new?"

"Didn't you hear? They are confiscating chairs from the Jews."

"What happened?"

"Hitler got tired of standing outside Moscow and Leningrad [a wry reference to the inability of Hitler's armies to conquer either city]."[76]

But in the ghetto laughter was fleeting; terror, an ever-present reality, routinely worked

A face peers through a window in a ghetto door. The sign reads in German and Polish: "Spotted Fever (typhus) Entering and Leaving Are Strictly Forbidden."

FLECKFIEBER
BETRETEN und VERLASSEN
IST STRENGSTENS VERBOTEN

DUR PLAMISTY
WSTĘP I WYJŚCIE
SUROWO WZBRONIONE

A homeless family, suffering from cold and hunger, huddles together on a Warsaw ghetto street. Jews suffered daily from Nazi brutality.

to undermine the optimism of more than a few ghetto dwellers. Halina Birenbaum, a survivor of the Warsaw ghetto, recalled that when she was ten years old

> the Nazis occupied Warsaw, and when the bestial terror began—our only reality—my mother used to calm me with the assurance that the Nazis' defeat was inevitable and close at hand, that I was not to be afraid, I must gather together all my strength and survive. . . .

> My mother listened with terror but also with distrust to news spread by refugees from the ghetto in the city of Lodz, of the inhuman cruelty and mass executions of local Jews. "They could not do that in Warsaw, they could not imprison and destroy a half-million Jews!"

> That was how my mother reasoned at first, and our neighbors thought the same. Doubting the truth of the nightmarish news, they comforted and encouraged each other, seeking refuge from a tragic and hopeless future.

> The streets of the Warsaw ghetto swarmed with beggars in lice-infested,

"A Quiet at Noon"

Large-scale action in the Warsaw Ghetto Uprising ended on May 16, 1943. German troops then began a systematic, street-by-street razing of every building left standing in the ghetto. In *The Holocaust: A History of the Jews of Europe During the Second World War*, historian Martin Gilbert includes a page from the diary of Leon Najberg, a Jewish survivor.

On May 19, while he and forty-four others were still in hiding, Najberg wrote:

> We are on the third floor and we have done away with stairs. We go upstairs with the help of rope-ladder. We are in burnt rooms, i.e. the Lidzbarski brother and sister, the Szarmans, the Koplows and so-called group of Klonski—it is ours. One floor lower there is the apartment of Tojst, quite saved with complete furnishings. I am looking at that apartment and see an analogy to present life of Jews. From among families there are—*for the present*—only individuals who saved their lives, from the whole streets which were occupied by Jews—individuals. . . . Though our hearts are still beating, there will never be a joy of life in them. . . .
>
> At 4 Walowa Street two bodies of new female victims lie and sun speeds up their decay and cats and crows eat up pieces of flesh from their faces. There was a quiet at noon.

Of the original group of forty-four, only Najberg and three others lived through the ordeal. Miraculously, they managed to escape the ghetto ruins and lose themselves in the non-Jewish section of Warsaw.

SS and German soldiers patrol the Warsaw ghetto after the Jewish uprising.

A woman mourns the death of a loved one as the funeral procession rolls through the Warsaw ghetto.

dirty rags. Whole families, swollen with famine, camped in hallways, gates and streets; dead bodies lay there, covered with newspapers or by snow in winter.

An epidemic of typhus broke out, accompanied by indescribable famine. The death rate was so high that it was impossible to keep up with taking the dead bodies away, and carting them to common graves in a cemetery.

Such were the conditions under which I grew up and learned to understand the world. I eyed the beggars, the starving urchins, the dead bodies in the streets, the carts moving through the ghetto carrying boxes into which they piled ten or more dead bodies at a time, so that the lids would not shut. . . .

I slowly stopped believing in my mother's assurances.[77]

And so suffered the little children in every ghetto in the land.

The Lodz Ghetto

The city of Lodz, located about seventy-five miles southwest of Warsaw, housed, after Warsaw, the second-largest Jewish community in prewar Poland. Lodz fell to the Germans one week after the start of World War II. In describing the German occupation of the city, the *Historical Atlas of the Holocaust* reports:

In early February 1940, the Germans ordered the establishment of a ghetto in the northeastern section of Lodz. Over 150,000 Jews, more than a third of the entire population of Lodz, were forced into a small area of the city. . . .

Living conditions in the ghetto were horrendous. Most of the area did not have running water or a sewer system. Hard labor, overcrowding, and starvation were the dominant features of life. The overwhelming majority of ghetto residents worked in German factories, receiving only meager food rations from their employers. More than 20 percent of the ghetto's population died as a result of harsh living conditions.[78]

Conditions in the surrounding villages and towns were no better.

Excesses

In late June 1940 the Germans sent Reserve Police Battalion 101 to Lodz as part of their effort to cleanse the area of Jews and make room for the relocation of German *Volk*. Bruno Probst [a pseudonym for a drafted reservist who took part in the operation] recalled the battalion's role:

In the resettlement of the native population, primarily in the small villages, I experienced the first excesses and killings. It was always thus, that with our arrival in the villages, the resettlement commission was already there. . . . This so-called resettlement commission consisted of members of the black[-uniformed] SS and SD as well as civilians. From them we received cards with numbers. The houses of the villages were also designated with the same numbers.

Children stare into the camera from the Jewish ghettos. The forced starvation and unsanitary conditions in the ghetto would lead to two thousand deaths a month in the Warsaw ghetto and eight hundred a month in the Lodz ghetto.

Will Work for Soup

Amid hardship and deprivation, Lodz ghetto dwellers exhibited many examples of Jewish ingenuity in their struggle to stay alive. In "Sketches of Ghetto Life: A Bowl of Soup," published in *The Chronicle of the Lodz Ghetto, 1941–1945*, Oskar Rosenfeld puts a new slant on working for one's supper. Rosenfeld, who lived the experience and captured the mood, writes:

> When something breaks down in the ghetto, it takes a great deal of time and effort to get it working again. . . .
>
> Say there's no water in the pipes. . . .
>
> Meanwhile, specialists are called in to fix the water pump. . . .
>
> Two strapping youths arrive. They examine and study the problem, and then tackle it. Soon you hear the snort of the motor, a noise that heralds the approach of water. A deceptive hope! There are a few drops in the pipe—[and then] the dream is over. The boys have left the scene.
>
> This game is repeated for several days. Is the repair work really so difficult, or is there some other reason for the delay?
>
> Then we learn that a workshop soup kitchen nearby uses the same water pipes. Naturally, our "hydraulics experts" are aware of this. And since they always receive a good gedakhte [thick] soup gratis whenever they come to do the repairs, they are not in any hurry. Every day, a bit of fixing; every day, a bowl of soup.

The cards handed to us designated the houses that we were to evacuate. During the early period we endeavored to fetch all people out of the houses, without regard for whether they were old, sick, or small children. The commission quickly found fault with our procedures. They objected that we struggled under the burden of the old and sick. To be precise, they did not give us the order to shoot them on the spot, rather they contented themselves with making it clear to us that nothing could be done with such people. In two cases I remember that such people were shot at the collection point. In the first case it was an old man and in the second case an old woman. . . . Both persons were shot not by the men but by noncommissioned officers.[79]

For members of Reserve Police Battalion 101, these "excesses" represented only the first of many to follow. History professor Christopher R. Browning reports:

> On November 28, 1940, the battalion took up guard duty around the Lodz ghetto, which had been sealed seven months earlier, at the end of April 1940, when the 160,000 [numbers vary] Jews of Lodz were cut off from the rest of the city by a barbed wire fence. Guarding the ghetto now became the major duty of Police Battalion 101, which had a standing order to shoot "without further ado" any Jew who ignored the posted warnings and came too close to the fence. The order was obeyed.[80]

This battalion of "ordinary men," as Browning calls them, soon established themselves as extraordinary killers.

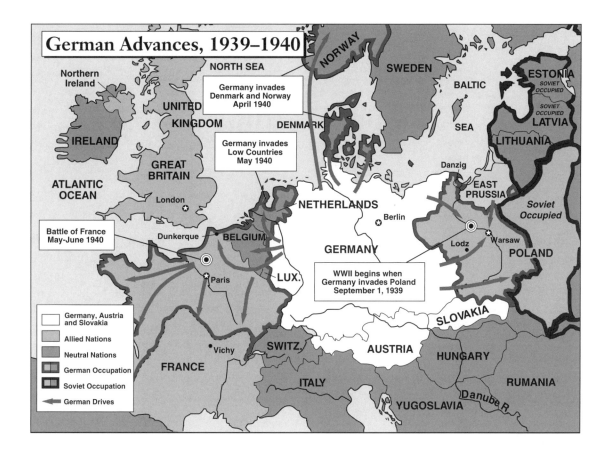

German Advances, 1939–1940

Northern Ireland
NORTH SEA
NORWAY
SWEDEN
BALTIC
ESTONIA *SOVIET OCCUPIED*
Germany invades Denmark and Norway April 1940
UNITED KINGDOM
SOVIET OCCUPIED
LATVIA
DENMARK
SEA
LITHUANIA
IRELAND
GREAT BRITAIN
Germany invades Low Countries May 1940
Danzig
ATLANTIC OCEAN
London
NETHERLANDS
EAST PRUSSIA
Soviet Occupied
Berlin
Battle of France May-June 1940
Dunkerque
BELGIUM
GERMANY
Lodz
Warsaw
POLAND
Paris
LUX.
WWII begins when Germany invades Poland September 1, 1939
SLOVAKIA
Vichy
SWITZ.
AUSTRIA
HUNGARY
FRANCE
ITALY
RUMANIA
Danube R.
YUGOSLAVIA

- Germany, Austria and Slovakia
- Allied Nations
- Neutral Nations
- German Occupation
- Soviet Occupation
- German Drives

Accelerating the Process

The German conquests in western Europe between April and June 1940—Norway, Denmark, Belgium, the Netherlands, Luxembourg, and France—brought another 436,700 Jews under the Nazi heel. And 77,000 Greek Jews fell under joint German and Italian control in April 1941. The Germans began to feel hard-pressed as to how to deal with the burgeoning Jewish population.

By June 1941 the death toll reached two thousand a month in the Warsaw ghetto, and eight hundred a month in the Lodz ghetto. By extension, however, if the Germans had allowed the third solution to continue unaided, it would have taken them about twenty years to eliminate the Jews through a process of slow starvation.

But the Germans were about to introduce a fourth solution to accelerate the process.

5 The *Einsatzgruppen:* The Special Killing Forces

On June 22, 1941, the Germans invaded the Soviet Union. Commencing with their latest aggression—code-named Operation Barbarossa—the Nazis ushered in the fourth and final time period of their war against the Jews. They also introduced a fourth and more expeditious solution to the Jewish question: Special mobile units called *Einsatzgruppen* (task forces) began the systematic killing of Jews in every locality in Russia, slaughtering as many as a million people in six months.

The aim of the fourth solution—after expulsion, emigration, and ghettoization—was to annihilate as many Jews as possible in the hundreds of small towns and villages throughout eastern Poland, Lithuania, Latvia, Estonia, and western Russia. In many cases, the Nazis wiped out entire communities in less than a half hour. The vigorous participation of local police and paramilitary groups helped to facilitate the killing. Meanwhile, the first three solutions remained actively in place.

The Commissar Decree

In March 1941, to prepare for the invasion of the Soviet Union, Hitler had issued the following order to his top military commanders:

> The war against Russia cannot be fought in knightly fashion. The struggle is one of ideologies and racial differences and will have to be waged with unprecedented, unmerciful, and unrelenting hardness. All officers will have to get rid of any old-fashioned ideas they may have. I realize that the necessity for conducting such warfare is beyond the comprehension of you generals but I must insist that my orders be followed without complaint. The commissars [Soviet Union government leaders] hold views directly opposite to those of National Socialism. Hence these commissars must be eliminated. Any German soldier who breaks international law will be pardoned. Russia did not take part in the Hague Convention and, therefore, has no rights under it.[81]

Although Hitler's military leaders harbored misgivings toward this order—popularly known as the Commissar Decree—in the weeks and months ahead they would carry it out to the letter.

Forming the *Einsatzgruppen*

On March 13, 1941, Field Marshal Wilhelm Keitel, chief of the German high command, issued five copies of a top-secret directive specifying a series of "orders for special areas," applicable to Operation Barbarossa.

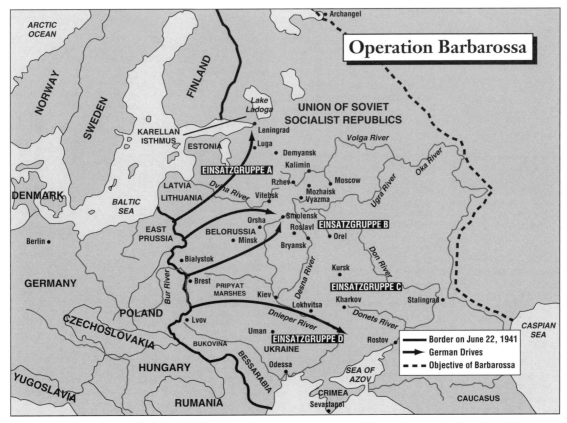

Operation Barbarossa

——	Border on June 22, 1941
→	German Drives
- - →	Objective of Barbarossa

His directive basically defined the roles, authority, and operational areas assigned to the armed forces, the SS, and the civil administration. One paragraph said, in part:

> In the area of army operations the Reichsführer-SS [Himmler] will be entrusted, on behalf of the Führer, with *special tasks* for the preparation of the *political administration*—tasks entailed by the final struggle that will have to be carried out between two opposing political systems. Within the framework of these tasks, the Reichsführer-SS will act independently and on his own responsibility.[82]

This paragraph, said to have been dictated by Hitler himself, gave enormous

power to Himmler and the SS. Himmler was to operate independently behind the battlefront, answering only to Hitler himself, while a task force of handpicked SS killers carried out the "special tasks" that would preface the last act in Hitler's war against the Jews.

At Himmler's direction, RSHA chief Reinhard Heydrich sounded a recruiting call that yielded volunteers from all departments of the SS. From a surplus of volunteers, Heydrich selected 3,000 men and organized them into four *Einsatzgruppen*, designated with the letters A through D: *Einsatzgruppe A*, comprising 1,000 men, was commanded by SS major general Franz W. Stahlecker and operated behind Army Group North in the Baltic countries; *Einsatzgruppe B*, with 655 men, was led by SS major general Arthur Nebe and worked to the rear of Army Group Central in the Russian Republic and parts of Belorussia; *Einsatzgruppe C*, numbering 750 men, was headed by SS colonel Emil Otto Rasch and operated behind Army Group South in the northern Ukraine; and *Einsatzgruppe D*, with 600 men, was commanded by SS general Otto Ohlendorf and covered the southern Ukraine, the Crimea, and the Caucasus to the rear of the Eleventh Army.

The four *Einsatzgruppen* were further split into nineteen subunits of *Sonderkommandos/Einsatzkommandos* (special units/killer units), each reporting to its parent *Einsatzgruppe*. Each *Einsatzgruppe* reported to one of four regional Higher SS and Police Leaders (HSSPF). The HSSPF, in turn, answered to the *Reichssicherheitshauptamt* (RSHA) in Berlin, which held the ultimate authority for the murderous *Einsatzgruppen* operations.

Beginning in May 1941 the *Einsatzgruppen* underwent training in recruitment centers located at Pretzsch and Düben in Saxony. In addition to routine military exercises, they were schooled in the specialized aspects of their assignment and groomed in the SS standard of athleticism, vigor, and strength.

Daily doses of Nazi dogma constituted not the least of their curriculum, including lectures on the inferiority of targeted "subhumans," principally, political commissars, Jews, and Gypsies. Reinhard Heydrich, for example, taught that "Judaism in the East is the source of Bolshevism and must therefore be wiped out in accordance with the Führer's aims." [83]

Intentionalists claim such assertions as further proof that Hitler intended from the start to eliminate the Jews. Conversely, functionalists insist that Hitler's "aims"—with regard to their implementation—had evolved and were still evolving. In either case, the

Members of the Einsatzgruppen *stand with suitcases and rifles. Such units were responsible for slaughtering as many as a million people in six months.*

four Einsatzgruppen followed the German armies eastward, and the extermination of the Jews moved from theory to practice.

Methods for Mass Murder

All along the vast eastern front that stretched from the Baltic to the Black Sea, the four *Einsatzgruppen* performed their tasks using remarkably similar methods in widely separated areas of operation. These similarities—methods that combined deception, terror, and orchestrated savagery—demonstrated that the officers and men of the *Einsatzgruppen* had learned their lessons well at Pretzsch and Düben. In a report issued on December 1, 1941, SS colonel

Karl Jäger, who headed *Einsatzkommando 3* of *Einsatzgruppe A*, described his procedure:

The decision to free each district of Jews necessitated thorough preparation of each action as well as acquisition of information about local conditions. The Jews had to be collected in one or more towns and a ditch had to be dug at the right site for the right number. The marching distance from the collecting points to the ditches averaged about 3 miles. The Jews were brought in groups of 500, separated by at least 1.2 miles to the place of execution. The sort of difficulties and nerve-scraping work involved in all this is shown in an arbitrarily chosen example:

In Rokiskis 3,208 people had to be transported 3 miles before they could be liquidated. . . .

Vehicles are seldom available. Escapes, which were attempted here and there, were frustrated solely by my men at the risk of their lives. For example, 3 men of the Commando at Mariampole shot 38 escaping Jews and communist functionaries on a path in the woods, so that no one got away. Distances to and from actions were never less than 90–120 miles. Only careful planning enabled the Commandos to carry out up to 5 actions a week and at the same time continue the work in Kovno without interruption.

Kovno itself, where trained Lithuanian [volunteers] . . . are available in sufficient numbers, was comparatively speaking a shooting paradise."[84]

In like fashion, Otto Ohlendorf, commander of *Einsatzgruppe D*, described a typical approach to operations conducted far to the south:

The unit selected would enter a village or city and order the prominent Jewish citizens to call together all Jews for the purpose of resettlement. They were requested to hand over their valuables and, shortly before execution, to surrender their outer clothing. The men, women, and children were led to a place of execution, which in most cases was located next to a more deeply excavated antitank ditch. Then they were shot, kneeling or standing, and the corpses thrown into a ditch.

Reinhard Heydrich soon found himself deluged with such reports from the east. Many were laced with bureaucratic doublespeak, such as "disposed of," "rendered harmless," and "seized." But some kept starkly to the truth, as in one report from *Einsatzgruppe A* in Lithuania, stating that "about 500 Jews, among other saboteurs, are currently being liquidated every day."[85]

In the summer of 1941, some Jews fled eastward with the Red Army, but most elected to remain in their homes. Their reluctance to flee prompted one German agent to report: "The Jews are remarkably ill-informed about our attitudes toward them. They believe we will leave them in peace if they mind their own business and work diligently."[86] By the end of 1941, close to a million Jews discovered the awful truth about the Germans and fell victim to the *Einsatzgruppen's* savagely efficient methods of mass murder.

"A Terrifying Nightmare"

One of the most brutal examples of *Einsatzgruppen* savagery took place in the town of Uman, near Kiev, in the Ukraine. It began on September 16, 1941, when members of *Einsatzgruppe C* posted a seemingly innocent public notice that said:

Women are forced to strip naked and walk to an open grave where they will be executed by the Einsatzgruppen. *Women with children were forced to carry them in their arms to a horrible death.*

Ukrainian militiamen commanded by SS officers had arrived. These militiamen had work tools with them and one of the trucks also carried chloride of lime.[88]

The Ukrainian militiamen dumped the chloride of lime next to the ditches to aid the rapid decomposition of corpses. Then a number of Junkers-52 transport planes landed at the airport, out of which emerged several units of SS soldiers. They marched up to the field-police unit and took up positions alongside it. With the *Einsatzkommandos* in place, the killing commenced. Said Bingel:

> One row of Jews were ordered to move forward and were then allocated to the different tables where they had to undress completely and hand over everything they wore or carried. Some still carried jewelry, which they had to put on the table. Then, having taken off all their clothes, they were made to stand in line in front of the ditches, irrespective of their sex. The *Kommandos* then marched in behind the line.
>
> With automatic pistols these men moved down the line with such zealous intent that one could have supposed this activity to have been their lifework.

Bingel stated that no one was overlooked:

> Even women carrying children two to three weeks old, sucking at their breasts, were not spared the horrible ordeal. Nor were mothers spared the terrible sight of their children being gripped by their little legs and put to death with one stroke

For the purpose of preparing an exact census of the Jewish population in the town of Uman and its subdistrict, all Jews, of all ages, must appear on the day appointed hereunder at the respective places of registration. Persons failing to comply with this order will be punished most severely.[87]

After reporting for the alleged census, the Jews were paraded off to a site near the Uman airport, where long ditches had been dug. Erwin Bingel, a regular army transportation officer, later described what occurred next:

> When the people had crowded into the square in front of the airport, a few trucks drove up from the direction of the town. From these vehicles, a troop of field police alighted and were immediately led aside. A number of tables were then unloaded from the trucks and placed in a line. Meanwhile, a few more trucks with

of the pistol butt or club, thereafter to be thrown on the heap of human bodies in the ditch, some of which were not quite dead. Not before these mothers had been exposed to this worst of all tortures did they receive the bullet that released them from this sight.

The slaughter lasted for nine hours. Row upon row of Jews went to their death amid cries of the children and the tortured. Finally, at 5 P.M., recalled Bingel,

> the square lay deserted in deadly desolation and only some dogs, attracted by the scent of blood in the air, were roving the site. The shots were still ringing in our ears. The whole thing might have seemed to me to be a terrifying nightmare but for the sparsely covered ditches which gleamed at us accusingly.[89]

An estimated 24,000 Jews perished at Uman that day. The men of *Einsatzgruppe C* continued their killing spree two weeks later at nearby Babi Yar, where—by actual count—they similarly murdered another 33,771 people.

Of Neurotics and Savages

The daily stress of face-to-face killing soon took a psychological toll on the gangs of *Einsatzgruppen* murderers. Rudolf Höss, who, as commandant of Auschwitz, knew all about mass killing, recalled:

> I had heard [Adolf] Eichmann's description of Jews being mown down by the *Einsatzkommandos* armed with machine guns and machine pistols. Many gruesome scenes are said to have taken place, people running away after being shot, the finishing off of the wounded particularly

Report from the Underground

One of the major disadvantages of the *Einsatzgruppen* mass-killing program, from a German point of view, was the inability to conduct it in secrecy. "A report sent out from Warsaw in May 1942 by the Jewish Labor Bund, then underground, to the Polish government-in-exile in London, was the first documentation to reach the West of the work of the Einsatzgruppen," writes Lucy L. Dawidowicz. In *The War Against the Jews, 1933–1945*, historian Dawidowicz includes a sampling of that report, which begins:

> Men from fourteen to sixty were rounded up in one place—a square or cemetery—where they were slaughtered, machine-gunned, or killed by hand grenades. They had to dig their own graves. Children in orphanages, inmates of old-age homes, and the hospitalized sick were shot, women were killed on the streets. In many towns Jews were taken away to an "unknown destination" and executed in the nearby woods. Thirty thousand Jews were murdered in Lwow, 15,000 in Stanislawow, 5,000 in Tarnopol, 2,000 in Zloczow, 4,000 in Brzezany (the town had 18,000 Jews, now has 1,700). The same happened in Zborow, Kolomyja, Stryj, Drohobycz, Zbaraz, Przemyslany, Kuty, Sniatyn, Zaleszczyki, Brody, Przemysl, Rawa Ruska, and other places. . . . According to various estimates, the number of Jews bestially murdered in the Vilna regions and Lithuanian Kaunas is put at 300,000.

Dina's Story

In late September 1941, the men of *Einsatzgruppe C* slaughtered almost thirty-four thousand Jews in a ravine outside Kiev called Babi Yar—Russian for "Old Woman's Gully." Dina Pronicheva miraculously survived the mass killings. Her story was told originally by Russian writer Anatoly Kuznetsov (aka A. Anatoli) and later included in Martin Gilbert's *The Holocaust*. Dina was shot and fell in the pit with all the others, and then:

> All around and beneath her she could hear strange submerged sounds, groaning, choking and sobbing: many of the people were not dead yet. The whole mass of bodies kept moving slightly as they settled down and were pressed tighter by the movements of the ones who were still living.
>
> Some soldiers came out on to the ledge and flashed their torches down on the bodies, firing bullets from their revolvers into any which appeared to be still living. But someone not far from Dina went on groaning as loud as before.
>
> Then she heard people walking near her, actually on the bodies. They were Germans who had climbed down and were bending over and taking things from the dead and occasionally firing at those who showed signs of life. . . .
>
> One SS-man caught his foot against Dina and her appearance aroused his suspicions. He shone his torch on her, picked her up and struck her with his fist. But she hung limp and gave no signs of life. He kicked her in the breast with his heavy boot and trod on her right hand so that the bones cracked, but he didn't use

> his gun and went off, picking his way across the corpses.
>
> A few minutes later she heard a voice calling from above: "Demidenko! Come on, start shoveling!"
>
> There was a clatter of spades and then heavy thuds as the earth and sand landed on the bodies, coming closer and closer until it started falling on Dina herself.
>
> Her whole body was buried under the sand but she did not move until it began to cover her mouth. She was lying face upwards, breathed in some sand and started to choke, and then, scarcely realizing what she was doing, she started to struggle in a state of uncontrollable panic, quite prepared now to be shot rather than be buried alive.
>
> With her left hand, the good one, she started scraping the sand off herself, scarcely daring to breathe lest she start coughing; she used what strength she had left to hold the cough back. She began to feel a little easier. Finally she got herself out from under the earth.
>
> The Ukrainian policemen up above were apparently tired after a hard day's work, too lazy to shovel the earth in properly, and once they had scattered a little in they dropped their shovels and went away. Dina's eyes were full of sand. It was pitch dark and there was the heavy smell of flesh from the mass of fresh corpses.
>
> Dina could just make out the nearest side of the sandpit and started slowly and carefully making her way across to it; then she stood up and started making little

foot-holds in it with her left hand. In that way, pressed close to the side of the pit, she made steps and so raised herself an inch at a time, likely at any moment to fall back into the pit.

There was a little bush at the top which she managed to get hold of. With a last desperate effort she pulled herself up and, as she scrambled over the ledge, she heard a whisper which nearly made her jump back.

"Don't be scared lady! I'm alive too."

It was a small boy in vest and pants who had crawled out as she had done. He was trembling and shivering all over.

"Quiet!" she hissed at him. "Crawl along behind me."

And they crawled away silently, without a sound.

Moments later, the boy warned, "Don't move, lady, there's Germans here!" Fortunately for Dina, the Germans did not understand the boy's words. She went undiscovered. But the Germans located the boy from the sound of his voice and killed him on the spot.

A Nazi SS commander lines up Kievan Jews outside a mass grave during the Babi Yar massacre. Note the Germans shooting victims in the neck before pushing them into the corpse-filled ditch.

the women and children. Many members of the *Einsatzkommandos*, unable to endure wading through blood any longer, had committed suicide. Some had even gone mad. Most of the members of these *Kommandos* had to rely on alcohol when carrying out their horrible work.[90]

Moments before his death and burial in a mass grave, a Jewish man seems to be patiently awaiting the final shot.

Even Erich von dem Bach-Zelewski, one of the top *Einsatzgruppen* generals, succumbed to the strain. In the fall of 1941, he shocked Himmler. After they had witnessed the execution of about a hundred Jews, he urged the *Reichsführer-SS*: "Look at the eyes of the men in this *Kommando*, how deeply shaken they are! These men are finished [*fertig*] for the rest of their lives. What kind of followers are we training here? Either neurotics or savages!" Shortly thereafter Bach-Zelewski himself was hospitalized with severe stomach and intestinal ailments. Dr. Ernst Robert Grawitz, chief SS doctor, diagnosed the maladies as "psychic exhaustion" and "hallucinations connected with the shooting of Jews" initiated by the general and "grievous other experiences in the East."[91]

By year's end the *Einsatzgruppen*'s mass-shooting methods proved to be unacceptable to the Germans. Such procedures were too slow and too hard to keep secret. Nor could they be applied in occupied territories in the west, where they would come under far greater scrutiny by the Allies. For these reasons, plus his grave concern over the adverse psychological effects on his killer elite, Himmler ordered his commanders to find a more humane method for processing large-scale executions.

Special Vans

"One of the methods chosen to circumvent the need to involve German soldiers in direct acts of killing," notes historian Leni

Where Sympathy Ended

Due to the nature of their murderous special tasks, the killer elite of Heinrich Himmler's *Einsatzgruppen* experienced many moral misgivings and psychological disturbances. American psychiatrist and author Robert Jay Lifton later interviewed a former Wehrmacht neuropsychiatrist who had treated many *Einsatzgruppen* members with psychological disorders. In *The Nazi Doctors: Medical Killing and the Psychology of Genocide*, Dr. Lifton relates what he learned from the German doctor:

> He told me that these disorders resembled combat reactions of ordinary troops: severe anxiety, nightmares, tremors, and numerous bodily complaints. But in these "killer troops," as he called them, the symptoms tended to last longer and to be more severe. He estimated that 20 percent of those doing the actual killing experienced these symptoms of psychological decompensation. About half of that 20 percent associated their symptoms mainly with the "unpleasantness" of what they had to do, while the other half seemed to have moral questions about shooting people in that way. The men had greatest psychological difficulty concerning shooting women and children, especially children. Many experienced a sense of guilt in their dreams, which could include various forms of punishment or retribution. Such psychological difficulty led the Nazis to seek a more "surgical" method of killing.

Dr. Lifton notes that such psychological problems "did not prevent those troops from murdering 1,400,000 Jews." Lifton also adds a telling footnote regarding the psychological difficulties of Erich von dem Bach-Zelewski, one of the top *Einsatzgruppen* generals:

> Himmler took a keen interest in the case of his "favorite general," conferring by telephone with [Dr. Ernst Robert] Grawitz, whom he severely chastised for failing to convey a full picture of Bach-Zelewski's condition and for what he considered the doctor's poor psychological treatment. Nonetheless, the general recovered sufficiently that a few months later he was back killing Jews as the newly appointed overall chief of anti-partisan formations in Russia. His breakdown had been in early March 1942. In September of that year, he wrote to Himmler recommending himself for the new position as the most experienced higher police leader. . . . As solicitous as Himmler was of Bach-Zelewski during his illness, the Reichsführer bristled when the general, at the time of his breakdown, asked whether the killing of Jews might be stopped in the East, and replied angrily, "That is a Führer order. The Jews are the disseminators of Bolshevism. . . . If you don't keep your nose out of the Jewish business, you'll see what'll happen to you!"

"For one who collapsed under his ordeal," Dr. Lifton concludes, "sympathetic therapy was the order of the day—until he could resume that ordeal. Sympathy stopped when the policy behind the ordeal was questioned."

"An Impression of Horror and Barbarism"

The mass murders perpetrated by the *Einsatzgruppen* could not be kept secret from regular German army units operating in the same areas. In *The History of the SS*, author and editor G. S. Graber includes an eyewitness report of SS atrocities from a major in the German Ninth Army to his commanding general. Dated January 3, 1942, the report reads:

At the end of July 1941 the 528th Infantry Regiment was in transit from the West to Zhitomir where it was to occupy new quarters. On the afternoon of the day we arrived there I moved into my staff HQ [headquarters]. From here we could quite clearly hear a large number of salvos followed by pistol shots which we decided must have been taking place nearby. I went to have a look, accompanied by the Adjutant and the Ordnance Officer. We got the impression that some cruel drama must be taking place. After a while we saw numerous soldiers and civilians streaming across a railway embankment, behind which, so we were told, firing squads were engaged in hectic activity. The whole time we could not see over the other side of the embankment, but every now and again we could hear shrill whistles which were followed by continuous machine-gunning. Some time later there were isolated pistol shots. When we had finally climbed up the embankment we saw a picture which, unexpected as it was, gave an impression of horror and barbarism. A grave had been dug into the soil, about seven to eight meters long [1 meter = 1.1 yards] and four meters wide. A pile of earth which had been dug to form the grave was at the side. This pile and the walls of the grave were absolutely sodden with streams of blood. The grave itself was filled with innumerable human corpses of all types and both sexes, so that one could not even guess at its depth. Behind the wall was a police unit commanded by a police officer. Their uniforms were spotted with blood. Round about, in a large circle, stood groups of soldiers who were already stationed there, some of them in bathing trunks; also numerous civilians with women and children. As I approached the grave I witnessed a scene which until this day I cannot forget. Among the corpses lay an old man with a white beard who still carried a walking stick over his left arm. He gave evidence of still being alive; he appeared occasionally to be trying to breathe. I asked one of the police officials to put an end to this man's life. The officer smiled at me and said: "I've already plugged him seven times in the stomach. Don't worry, he won't last much longer." The victims in the grave were not placed there in orderly fashion, they were simply left to lie where they had fallen. . . . During my service in the First World War, in the French and Russian campaigns of this war, I have never witnessed anything which had a more devastating effect on my spirit.

It is not known what the major's commanding general did with this information. Since the Wehrmacht was forbidden to interfere with *Einsatzgruppen* operations, he probably did nothing.

Yahil, "was the introduction of gas vans (*S-Wagen*, *S* = *spezial*)." She offers this description of the vans and their use:

A hermetically sealed compartment was mounted on the vehicle and the exhaust gases of the van were pumped in through rubber pipes [as with vans used earlier in the euthanasia program]. Up to sixty people—sometimes more—were jammed into the compartment. The victims were told that they were being transported to some other location for resettlement. The entire operation took fifteen minutes. However, this method did not solve the problem. Numerous hitches occurred and during the rainy season it was impossible to use the vehicles on muddy roads. Nor was this method any easier from a psychological point of view. The sight of the contorted corpses was so terrible that SS troops usually preferred the previous method of killing.[92]

Otto Ohlendorf, commander of *Einsatzgruppe D*, disapproved of the vans for another reason: While in their death throes, many of the victims evacuated their bodily functions, "leaving the corpses lying in filth," which caused his men to complain to him "about headaches that appear after each unloading."[93]

Dr. August Becker, an SS lieutenant and inventor of the vans, thought of himself as a humanitarian. Accordingly, he took steps to ease the victims' suffering and eliminate the resultant filth: He ordered the carbon-monoxide valves to be opened gradually rather than all at once, so that "prisoners fall asleep peacefully." The results pleased Becker: "Distorted faces and excretions such as could be seen before are no longer noticed."[94]

Despite such improvements, however, the vans could not handle the massive volume of executions required to keep pace with Himmler's demands. Jewish deportees from western Europe, the Balkans, and elsewhere, continued to arrive in the east in great numbers. And the advancing German armies continued to bring more and more Jews under German control. Used only briefly, the vans served chiefly as an interim bridge to a faster, more efficient, method of dealing with the burgeoning number of Jews in the east.

The Top War Priority

Beyond the problems associated with methods of mass murder, the *Einsatzgruppen* often encountered resistance from the Wehrmacht, primarily because of the army's need for forced laborers. Before the war, Jews had dominated industry and trade in many areas later occupied by the Germans. The army reasoned that the war economy demanded the use of all available workers, including Jews, to produce armaments and provide essential services. But the *Einsatzgruppen* insisted that the elimination of *all* Jews, even skilled workers, "was a matter of carrying out basic orders."[95]

The conflict of interest between the SS and the Wehrmacht was quickly elevated to Berlin for resolution. Berlin's terse response, dated December 18, 1941, removed all doubt as to the top war priority: "As a matter of principle, economic considerations should be overlooked in the solution of the problem."[96] Berlin's ruling came at a time when Germany's leaders were actively discussing still another approach to solving the Jewish question. Because their *fifth* solution intended the total annihilation of European Jewry, the Germans were already referring to it as the *final* solution.

Die Endlösung: The Final Solution

Lack of recovered evidence and the veil of history shrouds our knowledge of precisely when the Nazis first took formal steps leading to the Final Solution. But a few clues remain to guide us to an approximate start date.

Auschwitz, the largest concentration/extermination/forced-labor camp established by the Germans, was built in May 1940. Rudolf Franz Höss, the camp's commandant, would later testify before the International Military Tribunal (IMT) at Nuremberg that he had received orders from Heinrich Himmler in May 1941 to commence gassing inmates. And on July 31, 1941—as a captured Nazi directive later revealed—number-two Nazi Hermann Göring ordered concentration camp chief administrator Reinhard Heydrich to proceed as follows:

I herewith charge you with making all necessary preparations in regard to organizational and financial matters for bringing about the total solution of the Jewish question in the German sphere of influence in Europe. I further charge you to submit to me as soon as possible a draft showing the measures already taken for the execution of the intended Final Solution of the Jewish question.[97]

Heydrich later told associates that he had been entrusted with the task by Hitler himself.

The Wannsee Protocol

In the fall of 1941, Heydrich appointed *SS-Obergruppenführer* (lieutenant colonel) Adolf Eichmann as head of the Gestapo's Section IV B4 for Jewish Affairs (part of the RSHA), responsible for deporting Europe's Jews to extermination centers. Heydrich next convened a meeting on January 20, 1942, in the Berlin suburb of Grossen-Wannsee, to work out details for implementing the Final Solution.

Besides Heydrich, the conference was attended by fourteen other Nazi bureaucrats. They included Adolf Eichmann, who recorded the minutes of the meeting, and Gestapo head Heinrich Müller. The meeting lasted a mere eighty-five minutes.

Heydrich briefly reviewed the emigration problem. A plan for deporting all Jews to the island of Madagascar, which had been held as a reserve option, had been abandoned as unfeasible after the invasion of the Soviet Union. Instead of emigration, Heydrich told them, Hitler had sanctioned the evacuation of all Jews to the east as a "solution possibility."[98] After evacuation the Jews were then to be organized into huge labor

Children were not spared the horrors of the Holocaust. These Polish children were photographed upon their arrival at Auschwitz.

columns. In addition to being shot, beaten, gassed, starved, and frozen to death, the Jews could now look forward to being *worked* to death. (Functionalists point to both the Madagascar Plan and Hitler's sanctioning of evacuations as more proof that the Final Solution evolved through trial and error. Intentionalists insist that these were but *interim* steps leading to the total destruction of the Jews that Hitler planned from the beginning.)

Eichmann's notes of the meeting were later formalized and thereafter known as the Wannsee Protocol, excerpted as follows:

As a further possibility of solving the question, the evacuation of Jews to the east can now be substituted for emigration, after obtaining permission from the Führer to that effect. However, these actions are merely to be considered as alternative possibilities, even though they will permit us to make all those practical experiences which are of great importance for the future final solution of the Jewish question.

The Jews should in the course of the Final Solution be taken in a suitable manner to the east for use as labor. In big labor

Agents of Death

"Genocide requires two groups of people: a professional élite that formulates and supervises the killing, and professional killers who kill," writes noted American psychiatrist and author Robert Jay Lifton. In *The Nazi Doctors*, he describes both groups. Portions of his descriptions are shown here:

The Killing Professionals

Genocidal projects require the participation of educated professionals—physicians, scientists, engineers, military leaders, lawyers, clergy, university professors and other teachers—who combine to create not only the technology of genocide but much of its ideological rationale, moral climate, and organizational process. . . .

Hitler recognized the regime's need for particular professional groups, and its determination to make functionaries of those professionals; he issued a call to healers and thinkers to take leadership in destroying healing and thinking as they had known them. . . .

While the collective dynamic is working, individual professionals can feel themselves to be doing something earthshaking, "creating something new." . . . The dynamism of genocide offers considerable temptation to the professional to become the "spiritual engine" of change, revolution, renewal. . . .

The Professional Killers

The second, less educated group is likely to make up the "hit men" on the front line of the killing. They do the shooting or insert the gas pellets and their role, however diminished, is not eliminated in potential nuclear genocide. Rather than formulate principles or technology of killing, they act on these formulations and carry out the work. Limited in opportunities, they are likely to make killing their *only* profession; they become the artisans of killing, or the technologists of mass murder. . . .

They draw from a "corps spirit," the sense of shared combat of the most demanding kind. Their hardening is enormously stressed and related to cultural principles of masculinity (or sometimes feminine strength) as well as with a special commitment and self-sacrifice; in Himmler's term, not just ordinary soldiers but "ideological fighters." They are encouraged, and embrace the opportunity, to view their genocidal project as a military operation: one of subduing "partisans," as in the case of the *Einsatzgruppen*; or of "fighting" on the "racial battlefield" against the "dangerous Jewish enemy." . . .

Genocidal organizers are likely to combine corps spirit with literal mobilization of criminality. . . . Traditional criminality and corps spirit can of course be combined, as they were when the SS adopted a policy of welcoming criminals to its ranks and using them for murderous tasks. . . .

Men are drawn to these groups of professional killers by destructive psychological traits that can be considered psychopathic, but also by omnipotence and sadism, aggressiveness and violence.

gangs, separated by sex, the Jews capable of work will be brought to these areas for road building, in which task undoubtedly a large number will fall through natural diminution. The remnant that is finally able to survive all this—since this is the part undoubtedly with the strongest resistance—must be treated accordingly, since these people, representing a natural selection, are to be regarded as the germ cell of a new Jewish development, in case they should succeed and go free (as history has proved). In the course of the execution of the Final Solution, Europe will be combed from west to east.[99]

At a series of subsequent conferences, Heydrich and his fellow bureaucrats organized a system and the means to evacuate Jews en masse to concentration camps and extermination camps.

Day In Day Out

The Gestapo and the RSHA—particularly Adolf Eichmann's Jewish affairs and evaluation office—started channeling Jews eastward from locations throughout Europe at a gradually accelerating rate. In the midst of World War II, the Germans' systematic program for eliminating the Jews, once thought of as merely Hitler's political

Jews are boarded onto railway cars bound for concentration camps. Even though many Jews had heard rumors of the camps, they tried to hope for the best and believe the lies that the Germans told them.

rhetoric, now became an automated reality.

Adolf Eichmann later recalled that the massive movement of Jews to the east went more or less smoothly, and that he quickly became an expert in "forced evacuation."[100] While standing trial in Israel for war crimes in 1961, he described the system. Hannah Arendt, who covered the trial for the *New Yorker*, re-creates his description this way:

> There were hitches, but they were minor. The Foreign Office was in contact with the authorities in those foreign countries that were either occupied or allied with the Nazis, to put pressure on them to deport their Jews, or, as the case might be, to prevent them from evacuating them to the East helter-skelter, out of sequence, without proper regard for the death centers. (This was how Eichmann remembered it; it was in fact

not quite so simple.) The legal experts drew up the necessary legislation for making the victims stateless, which was important on two counts: it made it impossible for any country to inquire into their fate, and it enabled the state in which they were resident to confiscate their property.[101]

Eichmann, writes Arendt, explained that the Ministry of Finance and the Reichsbank (German national bank) provided facilities for receiving huge shipments of loot from all over Europe, including watches and gold teeth. The loot was then sorted in the Reichsbank and sent to the Prussian State Mint. The Ministry of Transportation supplied the needed railway cars, mostly freight cars, and arranged deportation schedules to avoid conflicts with other timetables. Eichmann or his agents notified the *Judenräte* of train quotas, and the Jewish councils furnished a list of Jews for deportation. Concluding Eichmann's description, Arendt writes:

Gold wedding rings taken from concentration camp victims testify to the vast number of Jews who perished in just one camp.

> The Jews registered, filled out innumerable forms, answered pages and pages of questionnaires regarding their property so that it could be seized the more easily; they then assembled at the collection points and boarded the trains. The few who tried to hide or to escape were rounded up by a special Jewish police force. As far as Eichmann could see, no one protested, no one refused to cooperate.[102]

Arendt ended Eichmann's description of the deportation system with a comment made by a Jewish observer in Berlin in 1943: "*Immerzu fahren hier die Leute zu ihrem eigenen Begräbnis.* [Day in day out the people here leave for their own funeral]."[103]

Web of Death

Preparations for the Final Solution included the establishment of an extermination camp in Chelmno—the first fixed gassing facility to become operational on more than an experimental basis. Using gas vans, the Germans began killing Jews and Gypsies from the Lodz ghetto on December 8, 1941. Figures vary, but some 320,000 people of the Warta River area died in Chelmno before the camp closed on January 17, 1945.

On May 27, 1942, Reinhard Heydrich, while serving as Deputy Reich Protector of Bohemia and Moravia, was critically wounded in Prague in a blast from a bomb rolled under his car by two British-trained Free Czech agents. Heydrich died from his wounds on June 4, 1942. But his legacy of terror and brutality lived on.

The assembly-line extermination of Jews in the General Government area had already begun, code-named Operation Reinhard in Heydrich's honor. Three more killing centers—Belzec, Sobibor, and Treblinka—were established to accommodate the victims of Operation Reinhard, the vast majority of whom were Jews deported from ghettos in Poland. Gassings, using carbon monoxide generated by stationary engines, took place in Belzec from March to December 1942; in Sobibor from April 1942 to October 1943; and in Treblinka from July 1942 to August 1943. Approximately 2 million Jews and others of the General Government area died in these three camps.

Two more death camps were established, one at Auschwitz, and one at Majdanek. Both camps also served as concentration/forced-labor camps. Auschwitz began operating as an extermination camp in March 1942; Majdanek, in October 1942.

Most of their victims were Jews transported from western, southern, and southeastern Europe. Of the 2.5 million Jews deported to Birkenau—part of the Auschwitz complex established for the extermination of Jews only—2.25 million were murdered there. Auschwitz alone, at the peak of its sinister productivity, housed more than 100,000 people. It was capable of gassing and incinerating as many as 12,000 victims daily. The United States Holocaust Memorial Museum estimates (conservatively) that 3.5 million Jews were killed in the six death camps as part of the Final Solution.

In all, the Germans established more than four hundred camp centers. Although some served only as transit and evacuation camps, each one represented a vital strand in Hitler's sprawling web of death.

A Typical Day

On a typical day in the death camps, SS officers greeted new arrivals, mostly Jews, at train and truck depots and selected the fittest for forced labor. The rest, including children, were sent at once to the gas chambers. At Auschwitz, the gas chambers could accommodate up to two thousand inmates at a time. Camp commander Rudolf Höss later described the grim inner workings at the camp:

> When I set up the extermination building at Auschwitz, I used Zyclon B [also spelled Zyklon or Cyclon], which was a crystallized prussic acid which we dropped into the death-chamber from a small opening. It took from 3 to 15 minutes to kill the people in the death-chamber, depending on climatic conditions. We knew when the people were dead because their screaming

Naked women and small children are led off to a massive pit to be executed. It is these kinds of photos, of women in the face of death attempting to comfort their children—to keep them from realizing the horrors that await—that are some of the most heartrending.

stopped. We usually waited for half-an-hour before we opened the doors and removed the bodies. After the bodies were removed our special commandos [*Sonderkommandos*, made up of prisoners who were partially trusted] took off the rings and extracted the gold teeth of the corpses.[104]

The Germans periodically killed the *Sonderkommandos*, a fate not unknown to them, and replaced them with Jewish prisoners selected from incoming transports. Yet, according to Höss, "they still did their job

with an eagerness and in a caring, helpful way," which, he said, always amazed him. One example of *Sonderkommando* behavior particularly impressed him:

As the bodies were being pulled out of one of the gas chambers, one member of the Sonderkommando suddenly stopped and stood for a moment as if thunderstruck. He then pulled the body along, helping his comrades. I asked the Kapo [slang for "foreman"] what was wrong with him. He found out that the startled Jew had discovered his wife among the bodies. I watched him for a while after this without noticing anything different about him. He just kept dragging his share of bodies. After a while I again happened on the work party. He was sitting with the others and eating as if nothing had happened. . . .

The way the Jews lived and died was a puzzle I could not solve.[105]

Inevitably, the sheer ghastliness of the daily mass exterminations exacted a toll on the perpetrators. Höss would often be asked by his men, "Is what we have to do here necessary? Is it necessary that hundreds of thousands of women and children have to be annihilated?" Upon reflection, Höss wrote:

And I, who countless times deep inside myself had asked the same question, had to put them off by reminding them that it was Hitler's order. I had to tell them that it was necessary to destroy all the Jews in order to forever free Germany and the future generations from our toughest enemy.[106]

Nor could Höss himself escape the whisperings of conscience:

Often at home my mind would suddenly recall some incident at the killing sites. That's when I had to get out because I couldn't stand being in the loving surroundings of my family. When I watched our children happily at play, or saw my wife bubbling with happiness over the baby, this thought often came to me: how long will your happiness continue? . . . Many a night as I stood out there on the railroad platforms, at the gas chambers, or at the burnings, I was forced to think of my wife and children without connecting them to what was taking place. The married men who worked the crematory or the open-pit burnings often told me that the same thoughts occurred to them. When they watched the women enter the gas chambers with their children, their thoughts naturally turned to their own families.[107]

Such was a typical day in the life of Rudolf Höss, who presided over the gas chambers and crematoria of Auschwitz for three and a half years. On April 7, 1947, Höss was executed at Auschwitz for his war crimes, beside the house where he had lived with his wife and five children.

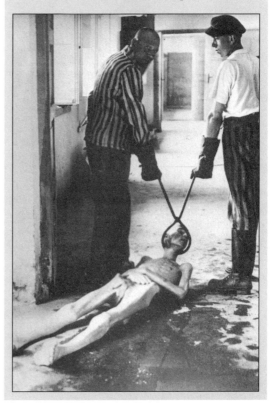

Jewish attendants drag the skeletal corpse of a man who died in the Dachau camp.

No Mercy Shots

In the early morning of November 4, 1943, the men of Reserve Police Battalion 101 murdered another fourteen thousand Jews. Again loudspeakers blared forth music to hide the sounds of gunfire. Christopher R. Browning, in *Ordinary Men*, excerpts group leader Martin Detmold's eyewitness description of the shootings:

> I myself and my group had guard duty directly in front of the grave.... From my post I could observe how the Jews . . . were forced to undress in the last barracks . . . then driven through our cordon and down sloped openings into the trenches. SD men standing at the edge of the trenches drove the Jews onward to the execution sites, where other SD men with submachine guns fired from the edge of the trench. Because I was a group leader and could move about more freely, I went once directly to the execution site and saw how the newly arriving Jews had to lie down on those already shot. They were then likewise shot with bursts from the submachine guns. The SD men took care that the Jews were shot in such a way that there were inclines in the piles of corpses enabling the newcomers to lie down on corpses as much as three meters high.
>
> . . . The whole business was the most gruesome I had ever seen in my life, because I was frequently able to see that after a burst had been fired the Jews were only wounded and those still living were more or less buried alive beneath the corpses of those shot later, without the so-called mercy shots. I remember that from out of the piles of corpses the SS [sic] were cursed by the wounded.

Harvest Festival

In October 1943 the Jews staged an uprising and attempted a mass escape at the Sobibor extermination camp. Jewish resistance had arisen earlier that year in Warsaw (April), Treblinka (July), and Bialystok (August). The Germans feared more such revolts in the General Government unless all the Jews assigned to forced-labor battalions were eliminated. And with German military reverses in North Africa and on the eastern front, Himmler recognized that the Wehrmacht might not be able to hold on to all the conquered territories. Time was running out for the successful completion of his task as supreme overseer of the Final Solution. He ordered the killing of all the remaining Jews in the General Government.

They code-named the action *Erntefest*—German for "Harvest Festival." The harvest comprised human lives and was not festive. It began at dawn on November 3, 1943.

The exterminators, men of the SS and Reserve Police units, surrounded the labor camps at Trawniki and Poniatowa. Jews were herded out of the camps in groups and shot in nearby pits, already prepared. Music blared from truck-mounted loudspeakers to hide the noise, but the sound of steady gunfire could still be heard. A similar scenario played out at the Majdanek death camp, where Jews were first separated from other prisoners, then led out to be shot in outlying trenches.

Heinrich Bocholt (a pseudonym for a member of First Company, Reserve Police Battalion 101) witnessed the shootings at Majdanek from about eleven yards from the graves:

> From my position I could now observe how the Jews were driven naked from the barracks by other members of our battalion. . . . [T]he shooters of the execution

Concentration Camps Throughout Europe

FINLAND

SWEDEN

NORWAY

North Sea

DENMARK

ESTONIA

U.S.S.R.

LATVIA

Baltic Sea

LITHUANIA

Sachsenhausen-
Oranienburg

Neuengamme

Ravensbrück

EAST
PRUSSIA

Stutthof

Bergen-Belsen

NETHERLANDS

Treblinka

Chelmno

Poland

BELGIUM

Gross-Rosen

Sobibor

Majdanek

Mittelbaudora
GERMANY

Flossenbürg

Auschwitz-
Birkenau

Belzec

Theresienstadt

Zweiler-
Struthof

CZECHOSLOVAKIA

FRANCE

Mauthausen

SWITZERLAND

AUSTRIA

HUNGARY

RUMANIA

Dachau

• Detention camps/Gestapo prisons

◉ Large-scale labor camps

▣ Large-scale extermination camps

Italy

YUGOSLAVIA

BULGARIA

Adriatic
Sea

Mediterranean Sea

commandos, who sat on the edge of the graves directly in front of me, were members of the SD. . . . Some distance behind each shooter stood several other SD men who constantly kept the magazines of the submachine guns full and handed them to the shooter. A number of such shooters were assigned to each grave. Today I can no longer provide details about the number of graves. It is possible that there were many such graves where shooting took place simultaneously. I definitely remember that the naked Jews were driven directly into the graves and forced to lie down quite precisely on top of those who had been shot before them. The shooter then fired off a burst at these prone victims. . . . How long the action lasted, I can no longer say with certainty. Presumably it lasted the entire day, because I remember that I was relieved once from my post. I can give no details about the number of victims, but there were an awful lot of them.[108]

Erntefest was completed in a single day. Some forty thousand Jews were exterminated, almost half of them at Majdanek.

Death Marches

The tide of war turned with the Allied invasion of Normandy in June 1944. By the following winter, advancing Russian troops started to threaten the death camp sites. Himmler and his cohorts had already begun entertaining second thoughts about the whole extermination program.

In November 1944 Himmler ordered the crematoria at Auschwitz destroyed, followed by the mass evacuations of Jews from the Auschwitz-Birkenau vicinity. Some one hundred thousand Jews died or were gunned down during these evacuations, which continued through the winter. Raizl Kibel, an Auschwitz survivor, later recalled her forced westward migration on one of the many appropriately named *Todesmärsche*, or death marches:

> In a frost, half-barefoot, or entirely barefoot, with light rags upon their emaciated and exhausted bodies, tens of thousands of human creatures drag themselves along in the snow. Only the great, strong striving for life, and the light of imminent liberation, kept them on their feet.
>
> But woe is to them whose physical strength abandons them. They are shot on the spot. In such a way were thousands who had endured camp life up to the last minute murdered, a moment before liberation.
>
> Even today I still cannot understand with what sort of strength and how I was able to endure the "death march" and drag myself to Ravensbruck camp, and from there, after resting a week or two, to Neustadt, where I was liberated by the Red Army.[109]

Although death marches occurred throughout the war, most of them took place during 1944 and 1945 to prevent the liberation of prisoners by advancing Allied forces. The evacuation of camps enabled the Germans to ensure a continuing supply of forced labor, and to delay discovery of war crimes. One of the largest marches was launched from Auschwitz. The Red Army entered Auschwitz on January 27, 1945, and freed about 7,000 remaining inmates, most of them ill or dying. Estimates place the death toll attributable to the death marches at about 250,000 victims.

Masters of the Situation

In October 1944, 650 Jewish boys from Hungary attempted to escape from Auschwitz-Birkenau but failed. Their German captors retaliated by gassing to death six hundred of the boys on October 20 of that year. Salmen Lewental, a member of the *Sonderkommando*—male Jews used mainly for body disposal—at Birkenau, recorded the fate of the boys in his notes. The following account appears in Martin Gilbert's *The Holocaust*, as Lewental wrote them in "the middle of a bright day":

> The boys looked so handsome and were so well built that even these rags did not mar their beauty.
>
> They were brought by twenty-five SS men, heavily burdened [with grenades]. When they came to the square the Kommandoführer [SS commando leader] gave the order for them to un[dress] in the square. The boys noticed the smoke belching from the chimney and at once guessed that they were being led to death. They began running hither and thither in the square in wild terror, tearing their hair [not knowing] how to save themselves. Many burst into horrible tears, [there resounded] terrible lamentation.
>
> The Kommandoführer and his helper beat the defenseless boys horribly to make them undress. His club broke, even, owing to that beating. So he brought another and continued the beating over the heads until violence became victorious.
>
> The boys undressed, instinctively afraid of death, naked and barefooted they herded together in order to avoid the blows and did not budge from the spot. One brave boy approached the Kommandoführer [standing] beside us . . . and begged him to spare his life, promising he would do even the hardest work. In reply [the Kommandoführer] hit him several times over the head with the thick club.
>
> Many boys, in a wild hurry, ran toward those Jews in the Sonderkommando, threw their arms around the latter's necks, begging for help. Others scurried naked all over the big square in order to escape from death. The Kommandoführer called the Sergeant with a rubber truncheon [club] to his assistance.
>
> The young, clear, boyish voices resounded louder and louder with every minute when at last they passed into bitter sobbing. This dreadful lamentation was heard from very far. We stood completely aghast and as if paralyzed by this mournful weeping.
>
> With a smile of satisfaction, without a trace of compassion, looking like proud victors, the SS men stood and, dealing them terrible blows, drove them into the [gas] bunker. The sergeant stood on the steps and should anyone run too slowly to meet death he would deal a murderous blow with the rubber truncheon. Some boys, in spite of everything, still continued to scurry confusedly hither and thither in the square, seeking salvation. The SS men followed them, beat and belabored them, until they had mastered the situation and at last drove them [into the bunker]. Their joy was indescribable. Did they not [have] any children ever?

Healing and Remembrance

While the liberating Allied armies surged across Europe from both the west and the east, the Germans tried to hide all evidence of their atrocities. Himmler called a halt to the Final Solution and sent out several peace feelers to the Allies. As a goodwill gesture, he started releasing Jewish prisoners for evacuation to Red Cross officials in Switzerland. His sick mind had led him to think that the Allies would endorse him as Germany's new leader, once Hitler was deposed at war's end. He thought wrong. Himmler took his own life with a cyanide capsule on May 23, 1945, while a prisoner of the Allies, rather than face war crimes charges.

Meanwhile, Russian troops liberated Warsaw and freed about 80,000 Jews in Budapest in January 1945. American forces freed 15,000 Jews at Buchenwald in April. The number of dead and dying and the starvation and sickness that they found shocked them greatly. British soldiers encountered similar misery when they released 40,000 prisoners at Bergen-Belsen, also in April.

Photographs taken by the liberators of Dachau, Buchenwald, Bergen-Belsen, and

Surviving inmates of Auschwitz celebrate the Russian liberation of their camp. These people were among the lucky ones that lived to see the end of their terrible ordeal.

One Day Too Late

In the spring of 1945, even as their world crumbled around them, the Germans persisted in their genocidal killing of the Jews. The *Todesmärsche*, or death marches, provided the Germans with still another method for eliminating Jews. In *Hitler's Willing Executioners*, Daniel Jonah Goldhagen cites, as an example, the experience of a survivor of a march from the Dora-Mittelbau camp:

> One night we stopped near the town of Gardelegen. We lay down in a field and several Germans went to consult about what they should do. They returned with a lot of young people from the Hitler Youth and with members of the police force from the town. They chased us all into a large barn. Since we were 5,000–6,000 people, the wall of the barn collapsed from the pressure of the mass of people, and many of us fled. The Germans poured out petrol and set the barn afire. Several thousand people were burned alive. Those of us who had managed to escape, lay down in the nearby wood and heard the heart-rending screams of the victims. This was on April 13. One day later the place was conquered by Eisenhower's army. When the Americans got there, the bodies were still burning.

Mauthausen for the first time conveyed proof of the atrocities to the West. Although these pictures did not depict the horror of the death camps, all of which had been destroyed by then, they were sufficiently horrific to stun the Western world. After visiting Buchenwald on April 21, 1945, a special ten-member group from Britain's Parliament reported

> that a policy of steady starvation and inhuman brutality was carried out at Buchenwald for a long period of time; and that such camps as this mark the lowest point of degradation to which humanity has yet descended. The memories of what we saw and heard at Buchenwald will haunt us ineffaceably for many years.[110]

There were, of course, as the world was soon to know, many "such camps as this," each with its own parcel of brooding memories.

The war ended on May 8, 1945. For Europe's Jews and countless other victims of the Nazi regime, the ordeal was over. The healing and remembrance was only beginning.

A New Chapter

The Allied victory in World War II lift-ed the mantle of German domination from continental Europe, much of which lay shattered and reshaped. Following Ger-many's unconditional surrender, the Four Power nations—Great Britain, France, the United States, and the Soviet Union—parti-tioned Germany and Austria into four sepa-rate occupation zones. The cities of Berlin and Vienna were similarly sectioned and occupied. And amid the crumbled ruins of Nuremberg, a medieval German city re-nowned for its toy makers, the Four Powers began the long and painful prosecution of the leaders of history's most evil regime.

The War Crimes Trials

Commencing on November 20, 1945, the Four Power nations brought twenty-two major Nazi war criminals before an Interna-tional Military Tribunal (IMT) to answer for their crimes. Notable among the defen-dants were Hermann Göring, the number-two Nazi; Ernst Kaltenbrunner, successor to Reinhard Heydrich as head of the RSHA; and Hans Frank, governor-general of Nazi-occupied Poland. The charges against them fell into one or more of three categories: crimes against peace, war crimes, and crimes against humanity. Adolf Hitler, the worst war criminal of all time; Heinrich Himmler,

overseer of the Final Solution; and Joseph Goebbels, propaganda minister of the Third Reich, all committed suicide and thus avoided Allied prosecution.

After a trial lasting more than ten months, the tribunal sentenced twelve defendants—including Göring, Kaltenbrun-ner, and Frank—to death, three to life imprisonment, and four to prison terms ranging from ten to twenty years. The IMT acquitted three defendants, and one—Robert Ley, head of the German Labor Front—hanged himself in his prison cell before the trial began. Göring swallowed a cyanide capsule to escape the hangman's noose. The other condemned men were hanged at Nuremberg on October 16, 1946.

Additional lesser trials were held in each of the occupation zones of Germany. Trials held in the U.S., British, and French zones alone resulted in the conviction and punish-ment of another 5,025 Germans between 1945 and 1949. At the same time, and dur-ing the ensuing decades, the countries of eastern and central Europe, and particularly the Federal Republic of Germany, conduct-ed, and continue to hold, similar trials.

During 1961–1962 Israel tried, convict-ed, and hanged Adolf Eichmann, head of the Gestapo's Jewish Affairs section (part of the RSHA). Eichmann had eluded the Allies

(From left to right, front row) Göring, Hess, von Ribbentrop, and Keitel are tried for various war crimes during the Nuremberg trials.

[lieutenant colonel] Eichmann, supreme arbiter of life and death. But the Eichmann I saw did not wear the SS uniform of terror and murder. Dressed in a cheap, dark suit, he seemed a cardboard figure, empty and two-dimensional.[111]

A dozen years after Eichmann was hanged, Wiesenthal admits having qualms about his execution: "When you take the life of one man for the murder of six million, you cheapen the value of the dead." But he later notes that "the Israelis were the judges. It was their affair."[112]

The Israelis initiated another much-publicized trial in 1987, when they accused John Demjanjuk, then a Ford Motor Company mechanic, of being the infamous "Ivan the Terrible," who operated the gas chamber at Treblinka. Demjanjuk was extradited to Israel and convicted but later released by the Israeli Supreme Court in 1993 when new evidence cast doubts on his guilt.

Still today trials are held in Europe and elsewhere. And they likely will continue to be held until the last member of the Nazi generation either is brought to justice or dies.

Of Bystanders and Brave Hearts

In the aftermath of World War II and during the more than half-century since its end, a virtual mountain of evidence has been accrued attesting to the entire panoply of Nazi war crimes. The forty-two-volume transcript of the first Nuremberg trials and the hundreds of captured Nazi documents entered into the trial records prove beyond question and without

after the war and fled to Argentina, where he was captured in 1960 by Israeli agents and returned to Jerusalem. His capture was due in part to a sixteen-year tracking effort by famed Nazi-hunter Simon Wiesenthal, who survived four-plus years in German concentration camps and who lost, except for his wife, his entire family to German atrocities. In his 1967 memoir, Wiesenthal recalls the first time he saw the man he had hunted for so long:

> There was nothing demonic about him; he looked like a bookkeeper who is afraid to ask for a raise. Something seemed completely wrong, and I kept thinking about it while the incomprehensible bill of indictment ("the murder of six million men, women, and children") was being read. Suddenly I knew what it was. In my mind I'd always seen SS *Obersturmbannführer*

Adolf Eichmann testifies during his 1961 trial in Israel. Eichmann had eluded justice by fleeing to Argentina after the war.

death marches. The seeming unreality of such a staggering figure strains the ability of most of us to fathom. And it begs an answer to a further question: While Hitler and his minions attempted to extinguish an entire race of people, how could millions of Germans (and others) stand idly by, neither raising a voice nor lifting a hand to stop them?

Many answers have been cited over the years, with collective apathy and fear of reprisal for protesting or resisting Nazi policy ranking high on the list of reasons. More now than before, historians point to the prevalence of anti-Semitism in the German culture. For example, Daniel Jonah Goldhagen asserts, "From the beginning of the nineteenth century, antisemitism was ubiquitous [present everywhere] in Germany. It was 'common sense.'" He goes on to state:

> The central image of the Jews held them to be malevolent, powerful, a principal, if not the principal, source of the ills that beset Germany, and therefore dangerous to the welfare of Germans. This was different from the medieval Christian view, which deemed the Jews to be evil and the source of great harm, but in which the Jews always remained somewhat peripheral. . . . This brand of antisemitism was usually violent in its imagery, and it tended toward violence. Its logic was to promote the "elimination" of Jews by whatever means necessary and possible, given the prevailing ethical restraints.[113]

It seems that in Nazi Germany the "prevailing ethical restraints" of which Goldhagen writes must have resided among the few and far between. The argument of what motivated bystanders to do nothing continues and cannot be settled here.

further recourse that the Holocaust happened. Revisionist denials or dilutions of such irrefutable evidence are, in a word, ludicrous.

Whether the Final Solution was planned by Hitler from the start and relentlessly executed by the Germans or whether it progressively evolved out of a system in chaos will probably never be established with certainty. Perhaps the eclectics come closest to the truth in opting for an answer somewhere in between.

In any case, some 6 million Jews, approximately one-third of the world's Jewish population at the start of World War II, perished in the concentration camps and ghettos, in the forced labor organizations, and on the

At the same time, however, we should remember that a few brave hearts *did* resist the Nazis and stood tall against their tyranny: members of the German Resistance inside Germany and members of various other resistance movements throughout Europe; guerrilla partisans in the outlands; and gentle people like the Dutch family in Amsterdam who sheltered Anne Frank, a fourteen-year-old Jewish girl, and her family from the Nazis for two years.

And we must never forget people like Raoul Wallenberg, a Swedish diplomat who almost single-handedly "saved between 30,000 and 100,000 [Jews] from certain death by issuing special passports, bribing guards and officials, interceding wherever possible, and often simply by bluffing."[114] Wallenberg was taken prisoner in Budapest by the Red Army in 1945 and disappeared into the Soviet Union. In 1991 a Soviet historian, although lacking documentary evidence, reported that Wallenberg had been shot as a spy in a Soviet prison two years after his capture.

Since courage often finds its reward in

Not all Germans complied with the Holocaust. These armed rebels are members of the resistance movement that fought to eliminate Hitler and his henchmen.

Jewish survivors of the war prepare to leave Germany for the promise of a homeland in Israel.

death, we might well speculate that bystanders will always outnumber the brave of heart by a wide margin.

Israel Reborn

Approximately 300,000 European Jews survived the Germans' attempt to exterminate them. Many of the survivors immigrated at first opportunity to the United States, Canada, the United Kingdom, South America, Australia, and Palestine. And between 1948 and 1951, almost 700,000 Jews immigrated to the newly established nation of Israel, including more than two-thirds of the Jewish displaced persons in Europe.

Although the Zionist movement toward establishing a modern Jewish State of Israel originated in the 1880s, the link between the Holocaust and the new Jewish homeland is clear. According to Holocaust historians Abraham J. and Hershel Edelheit, "The unprecedented nature of Jewish suffering during the Holocaust considerably speeded up the process that led to Israel's independence and the Jewish emergence from powerlessness."[115]

In their adopted countries, the Jews learned new languages and adopted new customs, while they tried to preserve their old cultures and heal their unhealable scars of continuing physical ills and psychological torment over the loss of loved ones. And above all—wherever they chose to begin life anew—they remembered that which they and humankind cannot and must not forget: Except for remembrance and eternal vigilance on the part of good people everywhere, the Final Solution could happen again.

Leni Yahil writes:

At the end of the war, a new chapter opened in the history of the Jewish people, with the establishment of the State of Israel taking prominence. . . . Alongside their longing for kin, their search for family and friends, and the strong desire to reconstruct their lives, they lifted their sights to the nation emerging in Palestine.[116]

Shalom aleichem! Peace unto you!

Notes

Introduction: Explaining the Holocaust

1. Quoted in Leni Yahil, *The Holocaust: The Fate of European Jewry*. Translated by Ina Friedman and Haya Galai. New York: Oxford University Press, 1990, p. 255.
2. Louis L. Snyder, *Encyclopedia of the Third Reich*. New York: Paragon House, 1989, p. 112.
3. Snyder, *Encyclopedia of the Third Reich*, p. 8.
4. Klaus P. Fischer, *Nazi Germany: A New History*. New York: Continuum, 1995, p. 497.
5. Daniel Jonah Goldhagen, *Hitler's Willing Executioners: Ordinary Germans and the Holocaust*. New York: Knopf, 1996, p. 9.
6. Goldhagen, *Hitler's Willing Executioners*, p. 9.
7. Abraham J. Edelheit and Hershel Edelheit, *History of the Holocaust: A Handbook and Dictionary*. Boulder, CO: Westview Press, 1994, p. 42.
8. Christopher R. Browning, *The Path to Genocide/Essays on Launching the Final Solution*. New York: Cambridge University Press (Canto edition), 1995, p. x.

Chapter 1: The Roots of Genocide

9. Adolf Hitler, *Mein Kampf*. Translated by Ralph Mannheim. Boston: Houghton Mifflin, 1971, p. 21.
10. Quoted in William L. Shirer, *The Rise and Fall of the Third Reich*. New York: Simon and Schuster, 1960, p. 25.

11. Quoted in Fischer, *Nazi Germany*, p. 88.
12. Fischer, *Nazi Germany*, p. 89.
13. Hitler, *Mein Kampf*, p. 56.
14. Hitler, *Mein Kampf*, p. 56.
15. Hitler, *Mein Kampf*, p. 56.
16. Hitler, *Mein Kampf*, p. 57.
17. Hitler, *Mein Kampf*, p. 57.
18. Hitler, *Mein Kampf*, p. 57.
19. Hitler, *Mein Kampf*, p. 58.
20. Hitler, *Mein Kampf*, pp. 58–59.
21. Hitler, *Mein Kampf*, pp. 61–62.
22. Robert S. Wistrich, *Who's Who in Nazi Germany*. London and New York: Routledge, 1995, p. 117.
23. Wistrich, *Who's Who in Nazi Germany*, p. 118.
24. Wistrich, *Who's Who in Nazi Germany*, p. 118.
25. Quoted in Robert Edwin Herzstein and the Editors of Time-Life Books, *The Nazis*. Alexandria, VA: Time-Life Books, 1980, p. 23.
26. Snyder, *Encyclopedia of the Third Reich*, p. 21.
27. Herzstein, *The Nazis*, p. 24.
28. Herzstein, *The Nazis*, p. 24.
29. Shirer, *The Rise and Fall of the Third Reich*, p. 185.

Chapter 2: The *Machtergreifung*: The Seizure of Power

30. Shirer, *The Rise and Fall of the Third Reich*, p. 4.
31. Quoted in Lucy S. Dawidowicz, *The*

War Against the Jews, 1933–1945. New York: Bantam Books, 1986, p. 48.

32. Dawidowicz, *The War Against the Jews*, p. 48.

33. Quoted in John Toland, *Adolf Hitler*. New York: Anchor Books, 1992, p. 291.

34. Shirer, *The Rise and Fall of the Third Reich*, pp. 4–5.

35. Quoted in Shirer, *The Rise and Fall of the Third Reich*, p. 5.

36. Quoted in Shirer, *The Rise and Fall of the Third Reich*, p. 5.

37. Alan Bullock, *Hitler: A Study in Tyranny*. New York: HarperCollins, 1991, pp. 146–47.

38. Bullock, *Hitler*, p. 149.

39. Shirer, *The Rise and Fall of the Third Reich*, p. 200.

40. Toland, *Adolf Hitler*, p. 309.

41. Edelheit and Edelheit, *History of the Holocaust*, p. 245.

42. Quoted in Yahil, *The Holocaust*, p. 60.

43. Yahil, *The Holocaust*, pp. 60–61.

44. Yahil, *The Holocaust*, p. 63.

45. Toland, *Adolf Hitler*, p. 310.

46. Quoted in Yahil, *The Holocaust*, p. 63.

47. Fischer, *Nazi Germany*, p. 282.

48. Edelheit and Edelheit, *History of the Holocaust*, p. 299.

49. Quoted in Toland, *Adolf Hitler*, p. 319.

50. Quoted in Fischer, *Nazi Germany*, p. 155.

51. Quoted in Shirer, *The Rise and Fall of the Third Reich*, p. 227.

52. Shirer, *The Rise and Fall of the Third Reich*, p. 227.

Chapter 3: The Doom of Jewish Life in Germany

53. Quoted in Snyder, *Encyclopedia of the Third Reich*, p. 346.

54. Quoted in Dawidowicz, *The War Against the Jews*, p. 69.

55. Dawidowicz, *The War Against the Jews*, p. 70.

56. Quoted in Dawidowicz, *The War Against the Jews*, pp. 86–87.

57. Quoted in Snyder, *Encyclopedia of the Third Reich*, p. 96.

58. Quoted in Toland, *Adolf Hitler*, p. 420.

59. Quoted in Shirer, *The Rise and Fall of the Third Reich*, p. 305.

60. Quoted in Shirer, *The Rise and Fall of the Third Reich*, pp. 306–307.

61. Fischer, *Nazi Germany*, p. 413.

62. Hannah Arendt, *Eichmann in Jerusalem: A Report on the Banality of Evil*. New York: Penguin Books, 1977, pp. 42–43.

63. Quoted in Arendt, *Eichmann in Jerusalem*, p. 46.

64. A. Read and D. Fisher, *Kristallnacht: The Unleashing of the Holocaust*. New York: Peter Bedrick Books, 1989, pp. 3–8.

65. Quoted in Shirer, *The Rise and Fall of the Third Reich*, p. 431.

66. Shirer, *The Rise and Fall of the Third Reich*, p. 431.

67. Quoted in Dawidowicz, *The War Against the Jews*, p. 106.

68. Fischer, *Nazi Germany*, p. 498.

69. Quoted in I. C. B. Dear and M. R. D. Foot, eds., *The Oxford Companion to World War II*. New York: Oxford University Press, 1995, p. 344.

Chapter 4: Slow Death

70. Dawidowicz, *The War Against the Jews*, pp. 199–200.

71. Edelheit and Edelheit, *History of the Holocaust*, pp. 342–43.

72. Dawidowicz, *The War Against the Jews*, p. 198.

73. Quoted in Snyder, *Encyclopedia of the Third Reich*, p. 97.

74. Quoted in Wistrich, *Who's Who in Nazi Germany*, p. 63.

75. Yahil, *The Holocaust*, p. 223.

76. Quoted in Dawidowicz, *The War Against the Jews*, p. 219.

77. Halina Birenbaum, *Hope Is the Last to Die: A Coming of Age Under Nazi Terror.* Translated by David Welsh. Armonk, NY: M. E. Sharpe, 1996, pp. 7–8.

78. United States Holocaust Memorial Museum, *Historical Atlas of the Holocaust.* New York: Macmillan, 1996, pp. 43–44.

79. Quoted in Christopher R. Browning, *Ordinary Men: Reserve Police Battalion 101 and the Final Solution in Poland.* New York: HarperPerennial, 1993, p. 40.

80. Browning, *Ordinary Men*, p. 41.

Chapter 5: The *Einsatzgruppen:* The Special Killing Forces

81. Quoted in Snyder, *Encyclopedia of the Third Reich*, p. 199.

82. Quoted in Dawidowicz, *The War Against the Jews*, p. 120.

83. Quoted in Dawidowicz, *The War Against the Jews*, p. 125.

84. Quoted in Dawidowicz, *The War Against the Jews*, pp. 127–28.

85. Quoted in Editors of Time-Life Books, *The SS*, vol. 2 of *The Third Reich* series. Alexandria, VA: Time-Life Books, 1989, pp. 122–23.

86. Quoted in Herzstein, *The Nazis*, p. 140.

87. Quoted in Herzstein, *The Nazis*, p. 141.

88. Quoted in Herzstein, *The Nazis*, p. 141.

89. Quoted in Herzstein, *The Nazis*, p. 142.

90. Quoted in Robert Jay Lifton, *The Nazi Doctors: Medical Killing and the Psychology of Genocide.* New York: Basic Books, 1986, p. 159.

91. Quoted in Lifton, *The Nazi Doctors*, p. 159.

92. Yahil, *The Holocaust*, p. 259.

93. Quoted in Herzstein, *The Nazis*, p. 141.

94. Quoted in Herzstein, *The Nazis*, p. 141.

95. Quoted in Dawidowicz, *The War Against the Jews*, p. 143.

96. Quoted in Dawidowicz, *The War Against the Jews*, p. 144.

Chapter 6: *Die Endlösung:* The Final Solution

97. Quoted in Rupert Butler, *An Illustrated History of the Gestapo.* London: Wordwright Books, 1992, pp. 110–11.

98. Quoted in Snyder, *Encyclopedia of the Third Reich*, p. 372.

99. Quoted in Snyder, *Encyclopedia of the Third Reich*, p. 372.

100. Quoted in Arendt, *Eichmann in Jerusalem*, p. 114.

101. Arendt, *Eichmann in Jerusalem*, pp. 114–15.

102. Arendt, *Eichmann in Jerusalem*, p. 115.

103. Quoted in Arendt, *Eichmann in Jerusalem*, p. 115.

104. Quoted in Snyder, *Encyclopedia of the Third Reich*, pp. 169–70.

105. Rudolf Höss, *Death Dealer: The Memoirs of the SS Kommandant at Auschwitz.* Translated by A. Pollinger. New York: Da Capo Press, 1996, pp. 160–61.

106. Höss, *Death Dealer*, p.161.

107. Höss, *Death Dealer*, p. 163.

108. Quoted in Browning, *Ordinary Men*, pp. 138–39.

109. Quoted in Gilbert, *The Holocaust*, p. 775.

110. Quoted in David Hackett, translator and editor, *The Buchenwald Report.* Boulder, CO: Westview Press, 1995, p. 11.

Afterword: A New Chapter

111. Quoted in Alan Levy, *The Wiesenthal File*. Grand Rapids, MI: Eerdmans, 1994, p. 135.

112. Quoted in Levy, *The Wiesenthal File*, pp. 136, 439.

113. Goldhagen, *Hitler's Willing Executioners*, p. 77.

114. Dear and Foot, *The Oxford Companion to World War II*, p. 1,254.

115. Edelheit and Edelheit, *History of the Holocaust*, p. 154.

116. Yahil, *The Holocaust*, p. 660.

Glossary

Aktion T4: Operation T4; code name for Hitler's euthanasia program, that is, the methodical killing of mentally or physically handicapped children and adults.

Anschluss: Germany's annexation of Austria in 1938.

Aryanism: Nazi theme of the supremacy of racially pure Nordics.

Babi Yar: A ravine outside Kiev; site of the mass slaughter of 33,771 people, mostly Jews, by the men of *Einsatzgruppe C.*

Beer Hall Putsch: Unsuccessful attempt by Hitler and the Nazis to overthrow the Weimar government in Germany in a Munich beer hall in 1923.

Commissar Decree: Hitler's authorization to murder Soviet commissars and others.

Die Endlösung: The Final Solution.

eclectic: One who supports the positive elements of both the functionalist and intentionalist viewpoints of the Holocaust.

Einsatzgruppe: A subdivision of the *Einsatzgruppen.*

Einsatzgruppen: Task forces; SS and police units assigned to the "special task" of killing Jews.

Einsatzkommandos: Killer units of the *Einsatzgruppen.*

Entjudung: De-Judaization, or getting rid of Jews.

Erntefest: Literally, "Harvest Festival"; code name for the slaughter of forty thousand Jews in occupied Poland on November 3, 1943, by men of the SS and reserve police units.

Final Solution: Nazi euphemism for the annihilation of the Jews of Europe; *Die Endlösung; see also* Holocaust.

Four-Year Plan: Hitler's plan to revitalize Germany's economy.

functionalist: One who believes that the Final Solution evolved, as opposed to having always been intended by Hitler and the Nazis.

Generalgouvernement: General Government; German name for Nazi-occupied Poland.

genocide: The deliberate and systematic destruction of a racial, political, or cultural group.

Gestapo: Secret state police; from *GEheime STAatsPOlizei.*

Gleichschaltung: "Coordination" process by which Hitler consolidated his power.

Holocaust: Name for the physical destruction of 6 million Jews during World War II; *see also* Final Solution.

Hossbach Memorandum: Document revealing first evidence of Hitler's aggressive intentions.

intentionalist: One who believes that Hitler and the Nazis always intended to annihilate the Jews of Europe.

Judenrein: Literally, "free of Jews"; a term used to denote the evacuation of Jews from towns and villages to make room for the re-settlement of ethnic Germans.

Kristallnacht: Night of the Broken Glass; Nazi rampage against Jews and Jewish establishments across Germany on the night of November 9–10, 1938, allegedly in retaliation for the assassination of a German diplomat in Paris by a Jewish youth.

lebensraum: Literally, "living space"; a phrase applied to Hitler's expansionist policy.

Machtergreifung: Seizure of power, which began with Hitler's appointment as Germany's chancellor.

Mein Kampf: My Struggle; title of Hitler's rambling, semiliterate autobiography.

Mischling: A part Jew.

Nationalsozialistische Deutsche Arbeiterpartei: National Socialist German Workers' Party; NSDAP—or later "Nazi"—for short.

Night of the Long Knives: Hitler-ordered purge of Ernst Röhm's SA by Himmler's SS resulting in a three-day bloodbath.

Nuremberg Laws of 1935: Two laws, the first stripping Jews of their citizenship and the second defining what constituted being a Jew.

Reichsbank: German national bank.

Reichstag: German parliament.

revisionist: One who attempts to change historical fact; for example, to deny that the Holocaust happened, or to diminish its consequences.

RSHA: *Reichssicherheitshauptamt;* Reich Central Security Office; the main security office of the Nazi government.

SA: *Sturmabteilung;* storm troopers; also known as Brownshirts.

Sonderkommandos: Special units employed for police and political tasks in the occupied Eastern Territories; more often a term used to describe Jews assigned to special work in concentration camps.

SS: *Schutzstaffel;* literally, "defense echelon"; an elite unit originally formed as Hitler's personal guard.

S-Wagen: Special vans designed to kill victims by pumping carbon monoxide gas into hermetically sealed compartments mounted on the vehicle.

Todesmärsche: Death marches.

Volk: Literally, "people"; racially pure German citizens.

Wannsee Protocol: Formalized minutes of the meeting convened by RSHA chief Reinhard Heydrich on January 20, 1942, to work out details for the Final Solution.

Wehrmacht: The German army.

Zionism: An international movement to establish a Jewish state in Palestine (now Israel).

Zyclon B: Crystallized prussic acid used in several of the death camps to kill Jews and others; also spelled Zyklon or Cyclon.

For Further Reading

Richard Breitman, *The Architect of Genocide: Himmler and the Final Solution.* New York: Knopf, 1991. A new study of the relationship between Himmler and Hitler that argues that it was Himmler who essentially laid the plans and devised the schemes for killing off the Jewish "race" in Europe and who was the true architect of genocide.

Henry Friedlander, *The Origins of Nazi Genocide: From Euthanasia to the Final Solution.* Chapel Hill: University of North Carolina Press, 1995. Explores in chilling detail how the Nazi program of secretly exterminating the handicapped and disabled and the exclusionary policies of the 1930s evolved into the systematic mass murder of Jews and Gypsies.

Anton Gill, *An Honourable Defeat: A History of German Resistance to Hitler, 1933–1945.* New York: Henry Holt, 1994. Drawing on recent research and on interviews with the few remaining resisters and their families, Gill tells the story of the Germans, small in numbers but great of heart, who secretly resisted the scourge of Nazism. The book serves as a primer on morality and human courage.

Eugen Kogon, *The Theory and Practice of Hell: The German Concentration Camps and the System Behind Them.* Translated by Heinz Norden. New York: Berkley Books, 1980. A true and detailed account of what life in the Nazi concentration camps was really like, written by a prisoner at Buchenwald who was a medical assistant to the Nazi doctor who conducted the infamous human medical experiments. It gives a picture—vivid, pitiless, and complete—of the systematic torture and murder of 6 million human beings.

Walter Laqueur and Richard Breitman, *Breaking the Silence: The German Who Exposed the Final Solution.* Hanover, NH: Brandeis University Press, 1994. The story of the German industrialist Eduard Schulte, who first warned the West of Nazi plans for the mass murder of Jews. "A remarkable picture of a bureaucracy of death and the unwillingness of one human being to countenance it."—Thomas Keneally

Deborah E. Lipstadt, *Beyond Belief: The American Press and the Coming of the Holocaust, 1933–1945.* New York: Free Press, 1993. A devastating indictment of the failure of the American press to report on the Holocaust; documents how our major papers ignored evidence of the Final Solution until after the war was over.

Callum MacDonald, *The Killing of SS Obergruppenführer Reinhard Heydrich.* New York: Collier Books, 1989. An in-depth account of the only successful assassination of a leading Nazi during World War II.

Ib Melchoir and Frank Brandenburg, *Quest: Searching for Germany's Nazi Past; a*

Young Man's Story. Novato, CA: Presidio Press, 1990. "Quietly astonishing . . . we catch his fire. Brandenburg's experiences offer chilling and incontrovertible evidence of a Holocaust once denied." —*San Francisco Chronicle*

D. Miklos Nyiszli, *Auschwitz: A Doctor's Eyewitness Account*. New York: Arcade Publishing, 1993. The author, a Hungarian doctor prisoner of the Nazis, was spared death to assist Nazi doctor Josef Mengele—the infamous "Angel of Death"—in his grim "scientific research."

Peter Padfield, *Himmler: Reichsführer-SS*. New York: Owl Books, 1993. "Peter Padfield's book on Heinrich Himmler is the first solid and readable account of Himmler's place and purpose as the most destructive of the Nazi leaders. It is a fine piece of historical work."—Telford Taylor

Joseph E. Persico, *Nuremberg: Infamy on Trial*. New York: Penguin Books, 1995. Persico describes the trial of the Nazi warlords of World War II in chilling character sketches and insightful observations about law and vengeance. According to a *Los Angeles Times* review, Persico's reconstruction of the trials that remain the model for judging international crimes "sometimes reads like a Ludlum novel."

Gerald Reitlinger, *The SS: Alibi of a Nation, 1922–1945*. New York: Da Capo Press, 1989. "[Reitlinger's] book, which reproduces all the nightmarish qualities of the Third Reich, provides abundant evidence that without the cooperation of the German bureaucracy and the tacit tolerance of a large portion of the German people, no SS, no Himmler, and no Hitler would have been possible."—*Christian Science Monitor*

Tom Segev, *The Seventh Million: The Israelis and the Holocaust*. Translated by Haim Watzman. New York: Hill and Wang, 1994. Shows the decisive impact of the Holocaust on the identity, ideology, and politics of Israel and reconsiders major struggles and personalities of Israel's past, including the Eichmann trial and the case of John Demjanjuk.

Gita Sereny, *Albert Speer: His Battle with Truth*. New York: Knopf, 1995. Sereny, one of Europe's foremost journalists, first saw Speer on trial at Nuremberg. Over the last years of the Nazi leader's life, she spent hundreds of hours in conversation with Speer and came to know him better than any other biographer. Of Sereny's rich and revealing work, Telford Taylor writes: "A totally absorbing and tremendously important book, an essential contribution to the history of the Third Reich, and of the individuals who managed it."

Albert Speer, *Inside the Third Reich: Memoirs by Albert Speer*. Translated by Richard and Clara Winston. New York: Galahad Books, 1995. Hitler's minister of armaments and war production takes a brutally honest look at his role in the war effort and trial at Nuremberg, during which he was the only one of the Nazis to admit guilt, providing a firsthand look at the inside of the Nazi state.

Tzvetan Todorov, *Facing the Extreme: Moral Life in the Concentration Camps*. Translated by Abigail Pollack and Arthur Denner. New York: Henry Holt, 1996. "A penetrating disquisition on good and evil . . . with rigor and grace Todorov reinvigorates the often tiresome debate over morality."—*Washington Post Book World*

Works Consulted

Hannah Arendt, *Eichmann in Jerusalem: A Report on the Banality of Evil*. New York: Penguin Books, 1977. Hannah Arendt covered the Eichmann trial for the *New Yorker*, where her report first appeared as a series of articles in 1963. For this revised edition of *Eichmann in Jerusalem*, the author has added further factual material that has come to light since the trial and a postscript commenting on the controversy that has arisen over her book.

Halina Birenbaum, *Hope Is the Last to Die: A Coming of Age Under Nazi Terror*. Translated by David Welsh. Armonk, NY: M. E. Sharpe, 1996. First published in Polish under the title *Nadzieja umiera ostatnia* by Czytelnik, Warsaw, 1967. A classic Holocaust reminiscence of the author's experiences growing up under the Nazis in the Warsaw ghetto, told in a clear, simple style that magnifies the horror of its content.

Christopher R. Browning, *Ordinary Men: Reserve Police Battalion 101 and the Final Solution in Poland*. New York: Harper-Perennial, 1993. The author tells the story of how a unit of average, middle-aged German policemen became the murderers of tens of thousands of Jews by taking part in the roundups and executions.

———, *The Path to Genocide: Essays on Launching the Final Solution*. New York: Cambridge University Press, (Canto edition), 1995. An authoritative account of the Nazi Jewish policy that seeks to answer some of the fundamental questions about what happened and why, between the outbreak of war and the emergence of the Final Solution.

Alan Bullock, *Hitler: A Study in Tyranny*. New York: HarperCollins, 1991. A comprehensive biography of the German dictator by a leading contemporary historian; thoughtful, clear, and well written.

Rupert Butler, *An Illustrated History of the Gestapo*. London: Wordwright Books, 1996. Perhaps the most comprehensive visual record to date of Hitler's dreaded henchmen, this volume shows more than 220 images chronicling the Gestapo's rise from a small Prussian police unit to a vast bureaucracy of terror. From the basement torture chambers to the sprawling death camps, this unflinching book provides a chilling look at the Reich's darkest depths.

Lucy S. Dawidowicz, *The War Against the Jews, 1933–1945*. New York: Bantam Books, 1986. An unparalleled account of the Nazi Holocaust—from the insidious evolution of German anti-Semitism to the ultimate tragedy of the Final Solution.

I. C. B. Dear and M. R. D. Foot, eds., *The Oxford Companion to World War II*. New York: Oxford University Press, 1995.

This single-volume masterwork on the greatest war in history contains "more than 1,700 entries—ranging from brief identifications to in-depth articles on complex subjects," bringing "the far-flung elements and events of the war into focus." The *Companion* includes detailed accounts of the Final Solution and related historical figures and events.

Lucjan Dobroszycki, ed., *The Chronicle of the Lodz Ghetto*. New Haven, CT: Yale University Press, 1984. A devastating day-by-day record of life in the second-largest Jewish ghetto in Nazi Europe—a community that was reduced from 163,177 people in 1941 to 877 by 1944. Compiled by inhabitants of the ghetto and illustrated with more than seventy haunting photographs, the *Chronicle* is a document unparalleled among writings of the Holocaust.

Abraham J. Edelheit and Hershel Edelheit, *History of the Holocaust: A Handbook and Dictionary*. Boulder, CO: Westview Press, 1994. This two-part history discusses in the first part the history of European Jewry, anti-Semitism, the rise and fall of Nazism and fascism, World War II, and the implications of the Holocaust. The second part provides a complete dictionary of terms relating to the Holocaust and a great deal of reference material on specific organizations, events, movements, publications, and other sources.

Editors of Time-Life Books, *The SS*, vol. 2 of *The Third Reich* series. Alexandria, VA: Time-Life Books, 1989. A lavishly illustrated and well-written chronicle of Hitler's elite force.

Klaus P. Fischer, *Nazi Germany: A New History*. New York: Continuum, 1995. This book, ten years in the writing, ranks right next to William L. Shirer's *The Rise and Fall of the Third Reich* for its comprehensive, richly narrated history of Germany during the Hitler years. Fischer sheds new light on the rise of National Socialism in Germany and on the problem of German "guilt."

Martin Gilbert, *The Holocaust: A History of the Jews of Europe During the Second World War*. New York: Henry Holt, Owl Books, 1987. Combines enormous historical research with the personal testimony of survivors, documenting not only what happened, but how and why the Holocaust occurred and why it can happen again.

Daniel Jonah Goldhagen, *Hitler's Willing Executioners: Ordinary Germans and the Holocaust*. New York: Knopf, 1996. "Goldhagen's astonishing, disturbing, and riveting book, the fruit of phenomenal scholarship and absolute integrity, will permanently change the debate on the Holocaust."—Simon Schama

G. S. Graber, *The History of the SS*. New York: David McKay, 1978. The author reveals aspects of the SS not widely known: the SS rituals, how the SS functioned as a business organization, and how the key SS men (Himmler, Heydrich, Eichmann, and others) operated within the SS—often against each other.

David Hackett, translator and editor, *The Buchenwald Report*. Boulder, CO: Westview Press, 1995. The first ever publication of army interviews with prisoners immediately following the camp's liberation in 1945; a remarkable and important document about the Holocaust.

Robert Edwin Herzstein and the Editors of

Time-Life Books, *The Nazis*. Alexandria, VA: Time-Life Books, 1980. A fascinating account of the Nazis and their evil culture before and during Hitler's twelve-year reign.

Adolf Hitler, *Mein Kampf*. Translated by Ralph Mannheim. Boston: Houghton Mifflin, 1971. The standard English-language translation of Hitler's autobiography.

Rudolf Höss, *Death Dealer: The Memoirs of the SS Kommandant at Auschwitz*. Translated by A. Pollinger. New York: Da Capo Press, 1996. An unexpurgated translation of the autobiography of history's greatest mass murderer; includes rare photographs, the minutes of the Wannsee Conference, original diagrams of the camps, a detailed chronology of important events at Auschwitz-Birkenau, and Höss's final letters to his family.

Alan Levy, *The Wiesenthal File*. Grand Rapids, MI: Eerdmans, 1994. An engrossing critical examination of the life and work of the Holocaust survivor and courageous hunter of Nazi war criminals.

Robert Jay Lifton, *The Nazi Doctors: Medical Killing and the Psychology of Genocide*. New York: Basic Books, 1986. The author, in his introduction to this agonizing account of physicians gone wrong, writes: "There are several dimensions . . . to the work. At its heart is the transformation of the physician— of the medical enterprise itself—from healer to killer. That transformation requires us to examine the interaction of Nazi political ideology and biomedical ideology in their effects on individual and collective behavior." Lifton's remarkable treatise stands unsurpassed as an examination into the darkest regions of the human psyche.

A. Read and D. Fisher, *Kristallnacht: The Unleashing of the Holocaust*. New York: Peter Bedrick Books, 1989. In Paris of 1938, a displaced seventeen-year-old Jew assassinated a Nazi functionary as an act of vengeance. Here is the story of *Kristallnacht*, the event that ignited the engine of the Holocaust.

William L. Shirer, *Berlin Diary: The Journal of a Foreign Correspondent, 1934–1941*. New York: Galahad Books, 1995. In this remarkable eyewitness account of Europe in the last half of the 1930s, William Shirer tells the story of a world in agony, slipping inexorably toward the abyss of war and self-destruction.

———, *The Rise and Fall of the Third Reich*. New York: Simon and Schuster, 1960. Published more than a generation ago, Shirer's masterwork remains the definitive history of Germany under Adolf Hitler. This book reads like a novel but presents the sinister story of the "thousand-year Reich" in unmatched detail.

Louis L. Snyder, *Encyclopedia of the Third Reich*. 1976. Reprint, New York: Paragon House, 1989. A definitive selection of historical information about Hitler and the Nazis.

John Toland, *Adolf Hitler*. New York: Anchor Books, 1992. The definitive biography of the man who disrupted more lives and stirred more hatred than any other public figure.

United States Holocaust Memorial Museum, *Historical Atlas of the Holocaust*. New York: Macmillan, 1996. A comprehensive delineation of Europe and the Nazi camp system between 1933 and 1950 compiled from archives around the world.

Robert S. Wistrich, *Who's Who in Nazi Germany*. London and New York: Routledge, 1995. Extensive information on the major figures who influenced life in Nazi Germany.

Leni Yahil, *The Holocaust: The Fate of European Jewry*. Translated by Ina Friedman and Haya Galai. New York: Oxford University Press, 1990. A sweeping look at the Final Solution, covering not only Nazi policies, but also how Jews and foreign governments perceived and responded to the unfolding nightmare.

Index

Picture Credits

Cover photo: National Archives

Archive Photos, 92

Archive Photos/American Stock, 44

Archive Photos/Anthony Potter Collection, 48

Archive Photos/Hackett, 71

Archives of the State Museum, Oswiecim/Courtesy of the Simon Wiesenthal Center Beit HaShoah Museum of Tolerance Library/Archives, Los Angeles, CA, 77

Bet Lohame Ha-Geta'ot/Courtesy of the Simon Wiesenthal Center Beit HaShoah Museum of Tolerance Library/Archives, Los Angeles, CA, 33, 93

Bildarchiv Preussischer Kulterbesitz/Courtesy of the Simon Wiesenthal Center Beit HaShoah Museum of Tolerance Library/Archives, Los Angeles, CA, 45, 59, 72

Bundesarchiv, 53, 57, 60

Bundesarchiv Koblenz/Courtesy of the Simon Wiesenthal Center Beit HaShoah Museum of Tolerance Library/Archives, Los Angeles, CA, 58

Corbis-Bettmann, 55, 83

Courtesy of the Simon Wiesenthal Center Beit HaShoah Museum of Tolerance Library/Archives, Los Angeles, CA, 40, 61 (bottom), 88

Der Stuermer, January 1934/Courtesy of the Simon Wiesenthal Center Beit HaShoah Museum of Tolerance Library/Archives, Los Angeles, CA, 20

Deutschland Erwacht/Courtesy of the Simon Wiesenthal Center Beit HaShoah Museum of Tolerance Library/Archives, Los Angeles, CA, 41

Ein Bilderbuch fuer Gross und Klein, Nuremberg, 1936/Courtesy of the Simon Wiesenthal Center Beit HaShoah Museum of Tolerance Library/Archives, Los Angeles, CA, 14

Hebrew Immigrant Aid Society/Courtesy of the Simon Wiesenthal Center Beit HaShoah Museum of Tolerance Library/Archives, Los Angeles, CA, 94

Library of Congress, 16, 18, 23, 25, 30, 37, 52

Main Commission for the Investigation of Nazi War Crimes, courtesy of USHMM Photo Archives, 82

National Archives, 11, 22, 26, 29, 34, 35, 49, 80, 91

Novosti/Corbis-Bettmann, 68

Stadarchiva Bielefeld/Courtesy of the Simon Wiesenthal Center Beit HaShoah Museum of Tolerance Library/Archives, Los Angeles, CA, 79

UPI/Corbis-Bettmann, 39, 47, 56

Yad Vashem Archives, 61 (top)

Yad Vashem/Courtesy of the Simon Wiesenthal Center Beit HaShoah Museum of Tolerance Library/Archives, Los Angeles, CA, 66

About the Author

Earle Rice Jr. attended San Jose City College and Foothill College on the San Francisco peninsula, after serving nine years with the U.S. Marine Corps.

He has authored twenty books for young adults, including fast-action fiction and adaptations of *Dracula*, *All Quiet on the Western Front*, and *The Grapes of Wrath*. Mr. Rice has written numerous books for Lucent, including *The Cuban Revolution*, *The O.J. Simpson Trial*, and seven books in the popular Great Battles series. He has also written articles and short stories, and has previously worked for several years as a technical writer.

Mr. Rice is a former senior design engineer in the aerospace industry who now devotes full-time to his writing. He lives in Julian, California, with his wife, daughter, two granddaughters, four cats, and a dog.